SEVEN WISE MEN
OF COLONIAL AMERICA

Seven Wise Men
of Colonial America

RICHARD M. GUMMERE

HARVARD UNIVERSITY PRESS

CAMBRIDGE, MASSACHUSETTS

1967

PREFACE

BOTH HISTORIANS and the general reader have agreed that the classical heritage of Greece and Rome played a large part in the ideas and activities of Colonial America, with a climax of interest at the end of the eighteenth century. The evidence is so convincing that the case may be stated rather than defended.[1] Careful investigation has proved that the classical tradition was, next to the Bible and the Common Law, a vital factor in provincial life and thought. The tradition was invoked by Captain John Smith when he appealed for Roman austerity in the formative days of the Old Dominion. It was deeply imbedded in the writings of Cotton Mather. We can follow it down through the works of a succession of provincial leaders in politics, theology, science, education, and literature up to the formal establishment of the United States. Its full bloom is seen in the old age correspondence of Jefferson and John Adams. Some of the tradition reveals itself in

[1] See Henry S. Commager, "Leadership in Eighteenth Century America and Today," *Daedalus,* 90:652-673 (1961). For a general view, see R. M. Gummere, *The American Colonial Mind and the Classical Tradition* (1963). Also Gerald F. Else, "The Classics in the New World," *News Letter* of the American Council of Learned Societies, vol. 16, no. 5, 1-6 (May 1965).

v

corporate action, as in the numerous compacts and tracts of the times. In the last analysis, however, it was the outspoken individual, in a long line of unusual men who were thinking their way into freedom and using the ancient material for their own purposes, who reacted to the Greco-Roman heritage. Nathaniel Ward, for example, was mainly responsible as a committee member of the *Body of Liberties* code of Massachusetts laws in 1641; but in his *Simple Cobler of Aggawam,* he spoke as an adventurous and entertaining writer whose humorous and trenchant style established him as a Colonial classic.

It should not be supposed that there were no protestants or abolitionists who held that the classics were over-praised and over-imitated by provincial Americans, and should cease to be regarded as an essential element in American culture. The historical critic should have his innings no less than the classicist. The honest sceptic who takes an impartial view, with some positive and specific concern in mind, will assess this Greco-Roman tradition at its proper value, and end by proving its importance.

I have selected a group of representative Colonials, who show no uniformity chronologically or geographically, and have no association with any one school of philosophy; all have frankly stated their opinions about their obligations to Greece and Rome. We shall let them tell their own stories, a chapter to each. We are following the principle that any effective organization profits by criticism and that, in the words of Cowper, "opposition gives opinion strength." The problem of classical influence on Colonial thought will be viewed from every angle. It is a curious fact that the least learned of these provincials made more use of the classical subject matter (in translation) than any of the trained scholars. These men should not be unfavorably compared with the great traditionalists; their contribution was outstanding, and they should not be regarded as *patres minorum gentium.*

If we follow these arbitrarily selected critics and commentators in their relationship to the issues and problems of our Colonial period, we shall find that they are apt to correlate them to the Greek and Roman tradition, whether pro or con. The classics serve as a frequent topic of discussion. Democracy, education, the march of science, slavery, capital punishment, religious freedom, the weakness of single legislative chambers, Deism and Arminianism, conflicts in medical and civic affairs, witchcraft, the importance of reading Latin rather than merely praising it, and the eternal problem of Whig versus Tory—all these cases are handled without gloves. In most instances the activity begins with the individual. In a word, there is little conformity and much controversy, as each man felt the challenge to his moral or cultural code. These worthies were not as conspicuous as the founders of colonies or the leading delegates to the Convention of 1787, or such pioneers as Winthrop and Penn. But each of them had a strong conviction that he must speak out his mind, whatever the details of his policy might be. They were nobly egoistic. Like Montaigne (who reeks with classical illustrations) they were original and vivid: "We can say that Cicero says thus, that these were the manners of Plato and these the very words of Aristotle. But what do we say *ourselves* that is our own? What do we do? What do we judge?".[2]

The close relationship of the present to the past aids the scholar and the reader of history in obtaining a better view of our Colonial culture. We may mention three outstanding witnesses to this fruitful partnership, whose statements command our attention. Emerson, in a happy epigram from his *Essay on Intellect,* remarked of himself: "I had a habit of tacking together the Old and the New."[3] The same thought,

[2] In his *Essay of Pedantry,* trans. Charles Cotton (London, 1700), third edition, p. 84.
[3] See also E. G. Berry, *Emerson's Plutarch* (Cambridge, Massachusetts: Harvard University Press, 1961).

expressed more "bookishly," had been developed by the picturesque bibliophile Isaac D'Israeli in his preface to the *Amenities of Literature*. He stressed the importance of such a partnership: "To be ignorant of all antiquity is a mutilation of the human mind—we but continue the chain of human sympathies, whose remotest link, be it ever so backward, supports whatever is now around us." A "third *wave*," as Plato defines the climax of Socrates' arguments, furnishes up-to-date evidence in the late George Sarton's *History of Science and the New Humanism*: "We shall be true humanists only to the extent of our success in combining the historical and the scientific spirit—There is no past, there is no future, simply an everlasting present. We all live in the present; but the present of the uneducated is narrow and mean, while that of a true humanist is catholic and generous. If the past were not part of your present, it were not a living past; it would be better for you to leave it alone."[4] In this way Sarton believed that he could teach any student "the cultural value of science, far transcending all its applications."

Many of our provincial leaders saw the importance of linking antiquity to the present day in both the sciences and the arts. Cotton Mather's activities included both natural history and theology. Franklin paid no less attention to his style of writing than to his practical experiments. Rittenhouse, who "read Newton's *Principia* in the English translation of Mr. Mott,"[5] was at home in Dutch, German, and French. James Logan, the classicist and botanist, two Winthrops, Cadwallader Colden, and William Bartram offer testimony to the interrelationship of the arts and explorations in the physical world,

---

[4] Bloomington: Indiana University Press, 1962; reviewed by I. B. Cohen in the *New York Times Book Review* (February 7, 1965).

[5] This is Andrew Motte, who published his translation of the *Principia* in 1729: *The Mathematical Principles of Natural Philosophy*. See Benjamin Rush, *Essays* (Philadelphia, 1806), p. 338.

with a classical background in many cases. In the world of letters the exchange was copious and regular.

In those days, when radio and rapid diffusion of information did not exist, there was much debate and controversy.[6] The provincials flourished on differences of opinion, both among groups and individuals. Pre-revolutionary Virginia and North Carolina were suspicious of one another. Sparks flew when representatives of each province gathered to determine the boundary line, with the uppish William Byrd of Westover caricaturing his Southern neighbors under fictitious mythological and astronomical nicknames. In Pennsylvania proprietary government versus the democratic policy of David Lloyd brought on continual clashes. The propaganda of Samuel Adams took the measure of Governor Hutchinson (an American-born official); and the withering satire of the Tory Jonathan Odell was matched by the brilliant buffoonery of John Trumbull. Old Dominion squires had to employ tutors for their sons; but the New England communities established their own grammar schools, with public support. Even in the field of pure literature, as well as in the unending theological quarrels, there were arguments and retorts, not always courteous. Amid such tensions, Benjamin Rush[7] offered this advice on the subject of immigration to America: "Men who are philosophers or poets, without other pursuits, had better end their days in an old country."

Some of the thinking evidenced by this group of seven wise men is parochial, some national, and some international. To most of them the classical tradition was an ornament, to others a tool. The conservatives still thought that the old grammar school, or the tutorial method, was the best preliminary for

---

[6] Charles R. Hildeburn, *A Century of Printing: The Issues of the Press in Pennsylvania, 1685-1784* (Philadelphia, 1885).

[7] Benjamin Rush, *Letters,* ed. L. H. Butterfield (Princeton: Princeton University Press, 1951), I, 550. *Essays,* p. 190.

the statesman or man of affairs as well as the theologian or *littérateur*. The radicals believed that the contents rather than the form were more important, and that the study of ancient languages should be confined to translations, or else limited to the final two years of school, and then only in case of preparation for law or medicine or other professions. Amid much debate and controversy there emerged some instances of exaggerated emphasis. These men made their contribution as independent individuals. We should respect but not idolize them. We may reduce them to size, but we must acknowledge their contribution to American life and thought.

R.M.G.

Cambridge, Mass.
April 1967

ACKNOWLEDGMENTS

The author offers his thanks and appreciation for editorial permission to reprint articles which have appeared in the following journals: *The Classical Journal,* October 1966, vol. 62, no. 1, pp. 1–8; *The Journal of Presbyterian History,* June 1962, vol. 40, no. 2, pp. 67–74; *Proceedings of the American Antiquarian Society,* October 1965, pp. 254–269. The poem by Emily Dickinson included in this volume is reprinted by permission of the President and Fellows of Harvard College and the Trustees of Amherst College; it is no. 371 in THE POEMS OF EMILY DICKINSON, edited by Thomas H. Johnson, The Belknap Press of Harvard University Press, Cambridge, Mass., copyright 1951 and 1955, by the President and Fellows of Harvard College.

For counsel and helpful advice, the author is deeply indebted to Samuel Eliot Morison and Howard Mumford Jones.

The author wishes also to record his appreciation of a further grant from the American Philosophical Society for final research assistance and preparation of the manuscript.

CONTENTS

I.   *The Reverend Hugh Jones:*   1
A Spiritual Pragmatist

II.   *Robert Calef:*   12
Critic of Witchcraft

III.   *Michael Wigglesworth:*   25
From Kill-joy to Comforter

IV.   *Samuel Davies:*   41
A Voice for Religious Freedom

V.   *Henry Melchior Muhlenberg:*   50
A Spiritual Trouble-shooter

VI.   *Benjamin Rush:*   64
A Classical Doctor's Dilemma

VII.   *Thomas Paine:*   81
Was He Really Anti-classical?

Notes   97

Index   109

A precious–mouldering pleasure–'tis–
To meet an Antique Book–
In just the Dress his Century wore–
A privilege–I think–

His venerable Hand to take–
And warming in our own–
A passage back–or two–to make–
To Times when he–was young–

His quaint opinions–to inspect–
His thought to ascertain
On them[e]s concern our mutual mind–
The Literature of Man–

What interested Scholars–most–
What Competitions ran–
When Plato–was a Certainty–
And Sophocles–a Man–

When Sappho–was a living Girl–
And Beatrice wore
The Gown that Dante–deified–
Facts Centuries before

He traverses–familiar–
As One should come to Town–
And tell you all your Dreams–were true–
He lived–where Dreams were born–

His presence is Enchantment–
You beg him not to go–
Old Volumes shake their Vellum Heads
And tantalize–just so–

Emily Dickinson

SEVEN WISE MEN
OF COLONIAL AMERICA

I

THE REVEREND HUGH JONES

A Spiritual Pragmatist

THE REVEREND HUGH JONES is a half-forgotten man whom historians are now beginning to recognize as a major contributor to the life and thought of his community. His *Present State of Virginia,* a critical but sympathetic view of the Old Dominion, published in London in 1724, ranks with the Journals of William Byrd and Robert Beverley's *History and Present State of Virginia.* He was a native of Herefordshire, bordering on Wales. In 1709, at the age of seventeen, he entered Jesus College, Oxford, proceeding to the B.A. in 1712 and taking priest's orders with a Master's degree in 1716. He applied to his Principal and to the Bishop of London for a position in Virginia and was appointed to the Chair of Mathematics and Natural Philosophy at William and Mary College.

Jones seems to have made good at the start. In 1718 he was named chaplain to the House of Burgesses and an assistant at Bruton Church. He taught physics, mathematics, and "Metaphysics" in the philosophical school of the college. He was on friendly terms with Governor Spotswood, whom he accompanied to several conferences with the Indians. Frank as always, he opposed Commissary Blair, disapproving his policy of allowing the vestries to select their ministers without consulting the governor. Jones was free with his advice, having the courage to criticize the mercantile monopolies of the London officials and the Board of Trade. He took an active part in the affairs of his community, discussing the proper age for children to share in the communion, the proper place for the pulpit, and the importance of a well-kept parson's glebe.

He returned to England for three years, married, and came back to Virginia in 1724. Perhaps because of his disputes with Blair, he moved to a Maryland parish, with the backing of Leonard Calvert, and settled for the rest of his life in that province at St. Stephen's Church, North Sassafras Parish, Cecil County, in the neighborhood of Bohemia Manor in 1731. He lived to a happy old age, leaving an estate of 858 pounds; he built up the church to a high degree of prosperity and influence. His death was reported in 1760.[1] His friendly relations with his congregation might have given circulation to the story that he left instructions to be buried with his feet pointed westward, in order to face his people as they rose from their graves on the Judgment Day: "he was not ashamed of them."

It is clear that Jones's scientific interests occupied much of his time and that his breezy but affectionate diagnosis of the young Virginians and their need for a less scholarly and more vocational program of study was a mere incident in his clerical and civic activities. His mathematical and astronomical attainments were considerable. The editor of the *Gentleman's Magazine* published in 1753 his "Panchronometer," or "Universal Georgian Calendar." In 1745 the same periodical had included his "Essay on the British Computation of Time, Coins, Weights, and Measures." He made some recommendations for the reformed calendar of 1752. He favored the octave rather than the decimal standard. Perhaps his most conspicuous role was that of the Chief Mathematician to the conferences on the Maryland-Pennsylvania boundary-line, which was not deter-

mined until the final survey by Mason and Dixon. He backed
Baltimore against the Penns and attacked the puzzling problem
of the Newcastle circle in drawing the boundary of Delaware.
Franklin printed an account of his "horizontal wind-mill," and
Jones was fascinated by the sage's electrical experiments.[2] He
was not in the least parochial. Besides wishing to install a
business school as a department of William and Mary College
(a plan which did not materialize), he suggested annual
scholarships to Oxford and Cambridge.

In addition to his *Present State of Virginia,* he published
a "Short English Grammar," which was to be "An Accidence
to the English Tongue," [3] and had planned two other tracts
—"Accidences" to Christianity and mathematics. The latter was
to include arithmetic, algebra, geometry, surveying, and navi-
gation. No copies of these last two texts are in existence, and
some think that they never reached the publication stage. There
is little quotation from the classics in any of Jones's writings.
His "English Grammar" (also published in 1724) contains
a much-used couplet from Horace's *Epistles:* [4]

> Si Quid novisti rectius istis,
> Candidus imperti; si non, his utere mecum,

(If you know anything better than this, share it frankly with
me; if not, make the most of it along with me.) The "Grammar" was especially recommended "for such boys and men
who have never learned Latin perfectly—for the benefit of the
Female Sex, and for foreigners."

In his *Present State of Virginia,* Jones evidenced no objection to the classical requirements for liberal arts colleges. He
was, however, sceptical of such offerings for those who were
not headed for higher learning. Many southern planters possessed a well-stocked library of the works of Plutarch and
other ancient writers, and Jefferson later insisted on a strict
classical equipment in the ancient languages for entrance into

his beloved University of Virginia. Nevertheless, business and politics were the main interests of the planters, and the average boy needed an academic program which would benefit him in his career. Jones, who knew his people well, emphasized the importance of practical training over a knowledge of Greek syntax and Latin texts.

Certain superior scholars, according to Jones, should have "the advantages of the College at Williamsburgh, where they may imbibe the principles of all human and divine literature, both in English and in the learned languages. But the majority of the youth, especially those who were educated in England, expose themselves to pedantic methods, too tedious for their volatile genius."

"The climate," Jones wrote, "makes them bright and of excellent sense and sharp in trade. . . . They have good natural notions and will soon learn arts and sciences. They are generally diverted by business or inclination from profound study and prying into the depths of things. . . .Through their quick apprehension they have a sufficiency of knowledge and fluency of tongue, though their learning for the most part be but superficial. They are more inclinable to read men by business and conversation than to dive into books. They are interested in learning what is absolutely necessary to the shortest and best method."

English, for example, might be a basic study "without going directly to Rome or Athens." The students might read masterpieces in translations (as many of them did). The experience of their teachers should be wider than "bare philosophy and speculative ethics. The educators of youth in Virginia should encourage them to be good scholars without becoming Cynics, and good Christians without appearing Stoics." On this basis the Old Dominion "could best serve the interests of Great Britain and the Colonies." Here the good Jones, besides giving academic advice for teenagers, is undoubtedly raising his objections against Deism—so popular at this time in England and Europe.

How far this educational missionary succeeded with his vocational propaganda is difficult to determine because by the middle of the eighteenth century a general American trend[5] in this "life-experience" direction began in many larger schools with the addition of practical courses to the curriculum. The indirect effects of Hugh Jones's educational theorizing can perhaps best be seen in the lives of two other distinguished southerners—George Washington and Henry Laurens.

Washington's career would have harmonized with the theories of Hugh Jones, had the latter lived long enough to observe the development of the "Pater Patriae." Washington carried out as an individual just what Jones regarded as the proper course of study for a representative Virginian who did not choose to be a candidate for college. With his "three R's" in elementary school, a flair for mathematics, and an apprenticeship under expert surveyors, we wonder how the self-taught future President acquired that logical and distinguished style, tinged with reminiscences of his reading in translations of the classics. We note in his writings a natural dignity of expression without any formal training in the technique of rhetoric. Washington often introduces a word or sentence in a figure of speech reminiscent of the classics and reflecting ancient history or mythology. In acknowledging the dedication of a tribute from a musical friend (Francis Hopkinson), we find Orpheus as the "type"; and during the French and Indian wars we note the countersign "Xanthippe"—a curious password for a regiment of soldiers. We may ascribe such references to Washington's realistic use of what he found in a few well-thumbed volumes. But fundamentally he studied for himself those subjects which Jones recommended as scientific or commercial.

At Belvoir, the home of his friends the Fairfaxes and particularly of the charming Sally, were some cherished volumes of essays on conduct, from which Washington filled a commonplace book, for the improvement of manners and morals.[6] He included quotations from Sir Roger L'Estrange's *Seneca's Morals by Way of Abstract*[7]—a sort of guide for ambitious career men. In this collection we find traces of memoranda calculated to make him more at ease in the company not only of William and Mary graduates but of British or European visitors.

Washington knew Addison's *Cato* almost by heart. North's *Plutarch* gave him much to think about and act upon. Among his many adages are some that are reminiscent of Seneca: "A good man can never be miserable;" "The contempt of death makes all the miseries of life easy to us." All these Stoic echoes are the distillations of his readings in ancient translations, reduced to usable size. There are, in the same tradition, traces of Marcus Aurelius.

In any case, painstaking reading with pen in hand and a definite goal of self-achievement were good companions to "the basic study of English" which Jones had recommended for the youth of Virginia. How deep an impression he made on provincial ideas of education is hard to determine, but he certainly cannot be called a *vox clamantis in deserto*. True, private tutors, whether local chaplains or college alumni, prepared their pupils for Oxford or Cambridge or an American college, and the regular classical program prevailed, in spite of Jones's warning against the sophistication of England and Europe. But a glimpse into the program of the non-collegiate teen-ager would indicate that the "Accidences" were worthy of consideration. The "Virginia dynasty" of American presidents, including Jefferson and Monroe from William and Mary, is an illustration both of Jones's precepts and of the strict classical program of the eighteenth century. The former group was typified by Washington, who continued his self-education, and the latter by Madison, who spent a graduate year at Princeton, studying classics and theology. These leaders would have satisfied both the academic and the vocational views of the Reverend Hugh Jones.

This Colonial clergyman would have pleased Henry Laurens with his educational theories, although we have no evidence whether or not the Charlestonian read Jones's *Present State of Virginia,* which appeared in London in 1724, the year of Laurens' birth.[8] From a gentleman apprenticeship in the family business, Laurens rose to the presidency of the Continental Congress. A practical statesman, who regarded the ancient languages as desirable only for those planning a profession and a college bachelor's degree, he would have found Jones's ideas congenial. He declared in a letter to a tutor: "The classics in my poor opinion have often been impediments to the success of young men, in an education of more value and utility *in the middle sphere of life."* [9] He was thus an opponent of the standard pre-university program as a requirement for the average boy; but he approved the Greco-Roman tradition as a cultural element in government, literature, and theology.

Laurens prospered as a merchant and was able to retire at the age of forty-seven. Politically, he aligned himself with the conservative wing of the patriotic party, and served his state in various capacities. His strict attention to business did not prevent him from taking an active interest in the cultural affairs of Charleston. He was elected to the American Philosophical Society before the Revolution, in 1771. In 1776, he was a delegate to the Continental Congress, and its president from November 1777 until December 1778. Subsequently, on his way to negotiate a loan from Holland, he was captured by a British ship, imprisoned and harshly treated in the Tower of London, and was finally exchanged for Cornwallis in December 1781. He limped away on crutches after his discharge, complaining with some justification about his treatment. He reached the American peace commissioners—Adams, Franklin, and Jay—in time to sign the preliminary treaty by the end of December 1782.

Laurens had been restive during his time in the Tower, and had copied large extracts from Gibbon as parallels to British domination, circulating them among friends of America. His clear-cut narration of his "Voyage, Capture, and Imprisonment" is praised as a model of descriptive prose by the historian M. C. Tyler.[10] A report by Lord Shelburne[11] to the British government describes him in partisan terms: "His early education was very limited; but when he became more affluent, by that unremitting attention which forms so remarkable a part of his character, he acquired a fund of miscellaneous literature. This fund is said to be ill-digested: it is rather a farrago." When a case in Charleston came into court concerning a condemned ship and the presiding judge, a relative by marriage, decided against Laurens, he circulated pamphlets attacking the decision. Shelburne calls him "sharp" in his dealings, especially in the American opposition to the Saratoga Convention, and prophesies that he will "outwit the British peace negotiators."

Before the Revolution began, Laurens had traveled in England and on the continent; as a Huguenot of French ancestry, he was happy in Geneva. Although occupied with a certain amount of business, he was chiefly interested in the education of his sons. The father's critical opinion of the classics did not prevent his younger son Harry from writing Latin verses at the Westminster School in London, or his elder son John, the brilliant and popular soldier-diplomat, from studying the usual humanities offerings in England and Geneva: "Latin, Greek, French, Italian, *Belles-Lettres,* Physics, History, Geography, Mathematics, Experimental Philosophy, Fencing, Riding, Drawing, and reading the Civil Law at the Middle Temple in London." [12] This was a large order, to be sure, and leads one to think that its breadth was greater than its depth. But the subjects were appropriate for an accomplished young statesman whose early death was lamented by a chorus of admirers, and prompted a special tribute from George Washington, on whose staff he had served.

The junior members of the family, including the daughter Martha, were more attracted to the ancient languages than was their father. Martha read regularly in the Greek New Testament, perhaps inspired by her husband, David Ramsay the historian. Her brother John Laurens may have known Homer in translation, or perhaps he hunted out an English version for his father's benefit; in a touching tribute he praised the senior statesman as Agamemnon praised Nestor, in the rendering of Chapman:[13]

> "Father, would to heaven that as thy mind remains
> In wonted vigor, so thy knees could undergo our pains.
> But age, that all men overcomes, hath made his prize
>   of thee;
> Yet still I wish that some young men, grown old in
>   mind, might be
> But in proportion of thy years and thy mind, young
>   in age,
> Be fitly answered with his youth, that still, where con-
>   flicts rage,
> And young men used to thirst for fame, thy brave
>   exampling hand
> Might double our young Grecian spirits and grace our
>   whole command."

The gist of this poetical wish, simplified in the enclosing letter, is clarified by John: "I wish, in the words of Agamemnon to Nestor, that we had ten such counsellors as you!" The son's summary is at least clearer than the ornate phraseology of Chapman—what Matthew Arnold called his "jogging rapidity."[14]

Both father and son had their doubts about slavery. The younger man, pondering its evils, uttered a general warning on the bad example of "the dangers of a too speedy manu-mission." Rome, he said, had suffered from swarms of freed-men who should have been given their liberty by a gradual process and after a checking of the record of the individual. [15] If we do a little sleuthing, we will find that the younger Laurens borrows from Seneca's forty-seventh *Epistle* (in a letter of 1765) about a certain unsatisfactory slave: "You say you don't like him; but remember he is a human creature whether you like him or not." John himself was defeated when he attempted to pass through the South Carolina Assembly a bill enfranchising the slaves, with the slogan of *ubi libertas, ibi patria,* holding that "the culture of the ground with us cannot be carried on without slaves; hence we should promote our slaves to freedom." [16]

Henry Laurens was a wide though not a deep reader, as Lord Shelburne noted. His classics came to him secondhand, and like most of his associates in Colonial affairs, he knew Rollin's *Ancient History* and some masterpieces in translation. He liked biography and travels. He confessed publicly that he did not understand Greek and was a "poor Latinist," and "not an adept in the dead languages." But he knew them well enough for practical purposes. For example, during the debate on subscribing to the Patriotic Association, Laurens humor-ously wondered whether the word *inimical* might not be too learned "for some of us in remote parts of the country who are not possessed of a Latin vocabulary."

We wonder where men like Laurens and Washington got their style of clear and forceful writing. We are on sound ground in the case of Washington; and to a certain extent, in the case of Laurens. The latter cared little for exact scholar-ship, inserting in his communications brief adages from ancient writings. During the vexing controversy prompted by the troublemaker Arthur Lee, he advised *Fiat justitia, ruat caelum.* One of his plantations was "Mepkin" (presumably an Indian word), staffed with devoted slaves named after luminaries in ancient history; and the name of another estate reflected his enthusiasm for a favorite author—"Mount Tacitus."

Typical family mottos were *Optimum Quod Evenit,* meaning "It happened for the best," and *Audiam Alteram Partem,* or "Let me hear the opposite opinion." When Drayton suggested a celebration on July 5th and a display of fireworks, Laurens replied that it should be a day of fasting: "The Olympic games of Greece and other fooleries brought on the dissolution of Greece." When he sought a proper epitaph for his son John, he rejected some hackneyed verses by the English poet Thomas Day, and turned to the Horatian tribute *Dulce et decorum est pro patria mori.*[17]

Henry Laurens cannot be defined as either a supporter or an opponent of the classics. He was simply a self-educated businessman and a statesman who took the classical tradition in his stride and at second hand. He at least understood the place of the classics in the intellectual life of his day, and in that respect serves well as an unwitting follower of the practical humanist Hugh Jones.

II

ROBERT CALEF

Critic of Witchcraft

THERE IS NO LOGIC or reason to be found in the annals of Salem Village and its environs from 1688 to 1692. The criteria were emotional as were the performers in the tragedy and many of the critics who have tried to explain it. The modern reaction to the events which took place is one of pity for the sorrows of the half decade of confusion and for what could be called a corporate nervous breakdown.

Our Colonial ancestors loved controversy. In the case of the Salem witch trials, the stage was set for a debate, with the Greco-Roman classics as a prominent topic for discussion. The details of the Salem episode are well known to every reader of American history. Those who wish to refresh their memories or renew their sympathy can dig as deeply as they wish into the bibliography which closes this article. The poet Whittier has dramatized the situation in his "Calef in Boston," where the representatives of "gown" and "town" speak their opinions in characteristically forthright terms:

> In the solemn days of old
> Two men met in Boston Town,
> One a tradesman frank and bold,
> One a preacher of renown–

Cried the last in bitter tone:
"Poisoner of the wells of truth,
Satan's hireling, thou hast sown
With his tares the heart of youth."
Spake the simple tradesman then
"Of your spectral puppet-play
I have traced the cunning wires.
Come what will, I needs must say:
God is true, and ye are liars."
But the Lord has blessed the seed
Which that tradesman scattered then,
And the preacher's spectral creed
Chills no more the blood of men.

The belief in witchcraft was widespread, and was subscribed to not only by the masses but by many persons of dignity and standing. *Maleficium,* or proof of witchcraft, was the final indictment to which there was no recourse. Although spectral evidence was ultimately rejected as improper testimony, and the trials were eventually and mercifully halted, the accusations, nevertheless, added up to a reign of horror. Unscrupulous troublemakers, both young and old, took advantage of the general panic, while serious scholars hunted for material on library shelves and in court records. There was an infinite variety of interpretation, and a conflict of personalities, prejudices, and enmities.

King James of England had published a *Daemonologie,*[1] and the example of England was contagious. Scotland was the scene of many hangings and burnings. Cotton Mather and to a lesser degree his father Increase wrote much about the history of the sinister art of witchcraft. There were only a few who spoke out frankly against the epidemic curse. Among them, to his everlasting credit, was Thomas Brattle, an American member of the Royal Society, who remarked that he "never thought judges infallible": they themselves could be misled by sorcery. John Wise of Ipswich risked his standing in the community by defending the innocence of the Procters in accord with his doctrine of individual rights. John Higginson of Salem disapproved of the trials while acknowledging the supposed existence of Satanic magic. Judge Samuel Sewall's manly confession, read aloud in the Old South Church five years after the investigations were stopped, was a touching apologia. The "still small voice" of Michael Wigglesworth commented on the sufferings of the victims: "I fear that innocent blood has been shed—families of such as were condemned for supporting witchcraft have been ruined by taking away and making havoc of their estates—the whole country lies under a curse to-day."

In general, the decisions of the judges seem to have been met by the community with a sort of semicredulous awe. Certain victims evoked sympathy and even tears. Cotton Mather tried psychiatry in hope of curing some of the afflicted. But too often the soul was thought to be in the power of Satan, and the individual was denounced as hopeless, as in the case of Martha Carrier, of whom the following is reported: "This rampant hag was the person who by the confession of the witches and of her own children among the rest, admitted that the Devil had promised her she should be Queen of Hell."

The old man Giles Corey enlists our particular sympathy. He was pressed to death by increasing weights piled upon him. The Reverend George Burroughs was fetched down from Maine by the sheriff and, on the evidence of the troublemaking young girls, who timed their fits by sessions of the court, was convicted of witchcraft. One of the complaints against him was based on his powerful physique: he could lift a seven-foot gun by inserting a finger behind the lock and holding the weapon like a pistol at arm's length. On the ladder he delivered a prayer which drew tears from those present, in spite of their belief in the validity of his conviction. Cotton Mather had remarked that it was "a righteous sentence." On one tense occasion a harassed citizen struck with his rapier at the likeness of the suspected Burroughs, as the soldier in Trimalchio's story had cut his way through crowds of invisible witnesses.

Testimony in the court and elsewhere sometimes bordered on insanity. The teen-aged mischief-maker Abigail Williams cried out in a crowded room that George Burroughs was bewitching the company in the form of a gray cat. A witness killed the cat, and it was reported that the coat of Burroughs was torn, presumably in the change from animal back to man. This and similar episodes, founded on superstition, would have been kept under control by some equivalent of psychiatry. But scientific investigation was then in its infancy; hence most of those convicted were martyrs and not criminals. Time, fortunately, has had its revenge. We are glad to learn that several descendants of the unfortunate George Burroughs have been leaders in their communities, as, for example, Isaiah Thomas, founder of the American Antiquarian Society.

There are plenty of explanations but few excuses for this period of sorrow and wholesale panic. Nathaniel Hawthorne, a lineal descendent of the remorseless trial judge, knew his Massachusetts history as well as anybody. He gives us a vivid impression of the Puritan mind, notably in his *Scarlet Letter*. Willful and stubborn personalities, a rough climate, the eeriness of the dark forest and the threatening Indians, the hardships of the almost frontier life, and the Puritan sense of sin which affected the politician, the minister, the scholar, and the working-man—these were vital ingredients in the picture. It was a matter of general concern to all except for a few well-to-do who kept the difficulties at arm's length and went about their business. We wonder why so few of the Proper Bostonians were involved, and their lack of involvement is to their credit. Both state and provincial affairs were in a state of confusion owing to such events as the tyranny of Andros and the much debated charter which Increase Mather brought back from England after four years of skillful diplomacy. It should be remembered that the older Mather was abroad during the most acute stage of the witch trials. The popular unrest, and the assumption that plagues and other ills were special marks of God's displeasure made up a formidable total of threats against the welfare of the province. It is clear that the Petronian proverb "Primus timor fecit in orbe deos" (It was fear that established the Gods on Earth) played a major role in Salem. Deodat Lawson declared in a sermon: "Audax omnia perpeti Gens Humana ruit per vetitum nefas." [2] (The human race, ambitious to try everything, is rushing to ruin with its forbidden crimes).

The two men who most actively debated the proper remedies for the lamentable situation in Salem were Cotton Mather and Robert Calef. The activities of the former are well known to historians and the general reader. Cotton Mather's approach was scholarly and fortified with reference to classical sources. He was a Fellow of the Royal Society, the author of the celebrated *Magnalia Christi Americana,* and a scientist who saw the importance of inoculation. He spoke authoritatively from his pulpit until the religious leaders of New England liberalized theology. The witchcraft problem attracted his attention and made him prominent. He devoted himself to the theory that witches should be exorcised by prayer and research. Hence his strenuous activity in the punishment of the deluded victims. From the ancient sources he drew many parallels which seemed to aim at a full understanding of the evil art of witchcraft and its abolition. He claimed an authority which we of today regard as misguided and sometimes tragic. The part he played in those perplexing days has provoked much discussion, but there is no doubt about what we might call his egoistic sincerity and his desire to lead the way against the forces of Satan.

Robert Calef was, however, a *novus homo,* in the Roman phrase, who emerged from obscurity to attack not only the witchcraft procedure and its superstitions, but also the habit of calling on Greek or Latin sources to bolster arguments. He was a pragmatist who felt that the only remedy for the witchcraft problem lay in a Christian approach and who took seriously his duties as a citizen. Born in England, he emigrated well before 1688, became a cloth merchant (some said a weaver), and was a selectman in Roxbury in 1697. He had previously recommended that a newcomer, Sir William Phips, should stop the Salem trials, for it was rumored that Phips and Lord Bellomont had "earned an accusation" because their wives got an accused woman discharged from custody. We today would have blessed their wives for their humanitarian efforts.

Calef had eight children; there are traces of the activity of Robert Calef, Jr., who often served as an assistant to his father. The senior Calef was an overseer of the poor, a constable in 1692, a clerk of the market, and a coroner's juror in 1692. He granted the existence and the power of witchcraft. As we shall see, however, he disapproved of its being a subject of theoretical and pagan learning. Sorcery should not be mixed with classical scholarship or magic mixed with religion. Calef had no hesitation in stating his opinion; in fact, he enclosed a copy of his *More Wonders of the Invisible World* in a letter to Lord Bellomont. This same work was publicly burned in the Harvard College Yard by order of President Increase Mather.

Calef was clearly a good and courageous citizen whose opposition to superstition should be recorded in his favor. The historian Thomas Hutchinson, whose ancestress was a victim of the Salem witch trials, stated "In his account of facts which can be evidenced by records and other original writings, Calef seems to have been a fair relator." [3] It was his conviction that

his leading opponent Cotton Mather was artificially and pedan-
tically putting a heathen label on a case which could be
solved practically by Christian means, without the aid of what
we today call psychiatry. Instead, however, the pagans were
summoned to corroborate miracles.

As early as 1684, Increase Mather published his *Essay for
the Recording of Illustrious Providences,* and later his *Cases
of Conscience Concerning Evil Spirits* (1698). Cotton Mather
had followed the paternal tradition of scholarship and religion
in his *Memorable Providences* (1689) and his *Wonders of the
Invisible World* (1693). The same themes are found in the
poetry of Benjamin Tompson, author of epics on the Indian
Wars, who quarried extensively from the last six books of the
Aeneid, in which mythology and the miraculous are combined.
All these publications were redolent of the classics. "Haec scrib-
ens studuit de Pietate mereri" (One's aim in writing these
books was the reward for dutiful devotion) was the watch-
word of the younger Mather. Both Mather and Tompson
felt that this Greco-Roman testimony was a guiding principle,
and that research in the ancient field could serve to emphasize
their message. The Reverend John Hale of Beverly, in his
Modest Enquiry, quoted Horace[4] and discussed the errors of
the Old Order: "Quo semel est imbuta recens, servabit odorem/
testa diu," rendered thus by a modern poet: "You may break,
you may shatter the vase if you will, but the scent of the
roses will cling to it still." He also warned the "enthusiasts,"
citing the ancient proverb "Felix quem faciunt aliena pericula
cautum."

In the debate over witchcraft and its relation to the classical
world, Cotton Mather represented the interests of the academic
scholars. Calef, on the other hand, took the part of the populace.
He recognized that ancient history and mythology were traditional fixtures which the "tradesman" regarded as superfluous.

Let us select some pertinent samples which the various au-

thors of *Memorable Providences* and other studies offer us
in great plenty, and which furnished material for the comments
of Calef. "The Devil," wrote Mather, has "mille nocendi artes"
(a thousand ways of doing harm). Among the miraculous
and harmful events described in Greek or Roman history and
mythology was the account of lightning striking without scorch-
ing. Even the bravest might be frightened by the thunderbolt:

Hi sunt qui trepidant et ad omnia fulgura pallent,
Cum tonat, exanimes primo quoque murmure caeli.[5]

(These are the men who tremble and grow pale at every
lightning flash: when it thunders, they quail at the first rum-
bling in the heavens.) Epicurus, however, was reportedly
skeptical about the effects of thunder: he declared that it came
from natural causes, and that awe in its presence was childish.

The old Roman code of the Twelve Tables was often cited
by the scholars. "They should not bewitch the fruits of the
earth, nor use any charms to draw their neighbor's corn into
their own fields." A typical beast-fable described talking animals and monstrous growths. The keel of the Argo and the
statue of Juno uttered human speech. The "Evil Eye," taken
from Pliny, was a frequent simile, describing persons who kill
people by merely staring at them. Cicero writes of women who
"had two apples in one eye that always did mischief with
their mere looks." This phenomenon may be compared to Ovid's
Pupula Duplex, or "the habit of fascination by a meer prolation
of words."

In both the spoken and the written word the academicians
alluded to ancient superstitions for illustration of witchcraft
activities. They had terms for all the charms and curses—"tot
sacramenta quot verba." "The Devil is that Vulcan, out of
whose forge came the instruments of our wars." He plans
earthquakes: "Deo permittente terrae motus causat." He is a
confederate of Medea,[6] who can charm the winds: "ventos

abigoque vocoque." Satan, like Proteus the Old Man of the Sea can change himself into many miraculous forms. The Devil's helpers can give superhuman strength to a mortal, as they did to the maiden Claudia who moved a ship grounded in the Tiber. They also inspired Tuccia to carry water in a sieve to prove her innocence.

The Church Fathers often called attention to certain apparitions reported in the classical writings in support of their own feelings about the connection between the devil and bewitched souls. They pointed out that Lactantius had held that "Demons can bring it about that non-existent ghosts may appear as realities to men." The influence of supposed ghosts and apparitions notwithstanding, Increase Mather had the courage to declare that "there is no more reality in what many witches confess than there is in Lucian's ridiculous fable of his being bewitched into an asse." Typical stories involved such figures as Salmoneus who had paid a penalty for his attempt to imitate the thunder and lightning of Jupiter: "Flammas Iovis et sonitus imitatur Olympi." [7] The Colonist Captain Davenport, killed by lightning as he lay asleep, was allegedly responsible for a *triste bidental*—a tabu-spot where the bolt struck. The were-wolf of Ovid's Lycaon; the destruction of snakes by incantation; incorporeal substances in the nether world; rain-charms, as in the showers which descended in answer to the prayer of Marcus Aurelius on his campaign among the Quadi—these were among the myths and legends gleaned from the classics. There were half-gods begotten by demons, nymphs beautiful but dangerous, and miracles such as those attributed to Vergil in the Middle Ages. We also find some Aristotelian phraseology or Plutarchian clausulae to an item of fiction, as in "This Concerning That."

Spells and charms figure frequently in the collection of miscellaneous *mirabilia* derived from ancient sources. The witch Canidia, as portrayed by Horace in his satires, is an ominous representative of her sinister art. She issued such warnings as:

> These dreams and terrors magical,
> These miracles and witches,
> Night-walking sprites or Thessalbugs[8]
> Esteem them not two rushes.

The love-charm verses sung by the shepherdess in the eighth Eclogue of Vergil also have their pseudo-tragic appeal; "Ducite ab urbe domum, mea carmina, ducite Daphnim," is a line of haunting beauty. The magic became more poignant: "As this clay hardens, so the traitorous swain, in the form of a waxen image, will melt away." The unhappy shepherdess makes up the image or "poppet," a figure bound with triple thread and carried twice round the altar. She has seen Moeris awake ghosts from the tomb and change to a wolf, a Lycanthropos. Another case which attracted notice both in Attica and in Cnidos, and was later alluded to by the Salem scholars, was that of a woman who "laid a spell upon Theodora that Callias might forget her!"

Especially dramatic were the "Ephesian Writings," or *Defixiones,* curses found in the house of the doomed Germanicus. The episode of the curses furnished grim gossip which the opponents of Calef disinterred from Tacitus the historian.[9] The results of this gossip took various forms in Salem village, from defamatory letters to crudely constructed poppets stuck with pins. The original narrative begins with an account of Piso's jealousy of the prince who supplanted him in the province of Syria. Piso's wife Plancina was accused of poisoning Germanicus. There was much mystery in the proceedings. Piso's illness in Syria, his death at Antioch in A.D. 19, and the backstage silence of the Emperor Tiberius fill out the tragic drama.

Tacitus's own words are: "Germanicus had a relapse, aggravated by his belief that Piso had poisoned him. The floor and the walls of his bedroom revealed the remains of human bodies, spells, curses, lead tablets inscribed with the patient's name, charred and bloody ashes, and other malignant objects which are supposed to consign human beings to the tomb." At the same time agents of Piso were accused of spying on the sick-bed. Ironic sequelae are mentioned by Tacitus. Agrippina carrying the ashes back to Rome, the crowds on the rooftops at Brundisium, and the widespread lamentation, enact a drama which ranks with any event in history.

The parallels taken from ancient sources and cited by Cotton Mather and other scholars were often overdrawn and out of place according to Robert Calef. "The Devil is not an independent power." Calef believed that only God is in control and the best means of combatting superstition is to follow Christian principles rather than to rely on secondhand classics. "An ancient author pretends to show the way, how a man may come to walk *Invisible*." But even the tract which the defending writer quoted is, according to Calef, a mere "Plinyism," an outworn relic of pre-Christian doctrines. Calef rebuked the responsible parties for stirring up superstitions which "Savor so much of Pythagoras's transmigration of souls—that a body may be at the same time in several places."

"It were too Icarian a task," declared Calef, "for one furnished with necessary learning and library to give any just account from whence so great delusions have sprung." Here was the opinion of a man who was not attacking the classics so much as he was objecting to the *abuse* of the classics. The scene at Salem was no place for any historian or philosopher of ancient times. The witch trials were the work of Satan, a temporary phase of the Devil's activity. In mentioning Sir William Phips, Calef gives his own definition of the tragedy: "If there was in these actions an angel supervising, there is little reason to think it was Gabriel, or the spirit of Mercury, nor Hanael the angel or spirit of Venus, nor yet Samuel the angel or spirit of Mars—names feigned by the said Trithemius,[10] etc. It may rather be thought to be Apollyon or Abaddon." [11]

Calef believed that there was a danger in exposing children to pagan untruths, and a grave error in making heathen writings the material of a clergyman's education. "As long as men suffer themselves to be poisoned in their education and be grounded in a false belief by the books of the heathen, so long will God be daily dishonored." Calef quotes Jean Bodin with strong disapproval. Bodin's tale of "an egg which a writer sold to an Englishman and by magic transformed him into an ass, and made him a market-mule for three years, to ride on and to buy butter, and how at last he was metamorphosed into the native shape of a man again" is a curious reflection from Apuleius, awkwardly presented by Calef in his preface to *More Wonders of the Invisible World*.

Calef's main aim was to emphasize the error of utilizing pagan testimony in a situation where Christian ethics should have been the criterion and the remedy for the sins of 1692. He goes to extremes in denouncing "the pernicious words of pagan learning in Vergil, Horace, Ovid, and Homer," and defends his stand by referring to Justin Martyr's attack on the credibility of the *telesmata* (talismans) of the magician Apollonius of Tyana.[12]

Whether Calef had any part in leading Judge Sewall to his confession of 1697, is impossible to decide. But he speaks out clearly enough: "Thus, Sir, I have given you a genuine account of my sentiments and actions in this affair; and do request that, if I err, I may be shewed it from Scripture or sound reasoning and not by quotations out of Vergil nor Spanish rhetoric[13]—These writers cannot pretend to shew a distinction between witchcraft in the common notion of it, and *possession*." [14]

In the debates concerning witchcraft, taking for granted the horrors and injustices of a lustrum of panic, we find that the classics play a part on both sides. In the one case, they are exhibited as research aids to the study of witchcraft, drawing on many centuries of investigation. In the other case, a man of business, working up some classical illustrations only to knock them down, regards them as inadequate to the problem and better expressed in the language of Christianity. This is the kernel of the controversy: the sorrows, the cruelty, the pathetic forced testimony dealing often with underprivileged victims, culminating in twenty-one executions, excite our sympathy and our indignation. In this mood we should leave the sufferers and try to understand the blot on the 'scutcheon which both sides have endeavored to wipe clear.

III

MICHAEL WIGGLESWORTH

From Kill-joy to Comforter

MICHAEL WIGGLESWORTH has suffered at the hands of American scholars and critics because his poem *The Day of Doom,* with its thesis of predestinated brimstone and eternal punishment for sinners, has been regarded as the conspicuous accomplishment of his career. Perhaps it was: for the general reader turns first to this Puritan "best seller," with its merciless story of saintly self-satisfaction as contrasted with the tortures of the damned. The reader is apt to interpret the book not as a reflection of the times, but as a brutal presentation of Calvinism at its strictest. In his "Postscript" to *The Day of Doom,* Wigglesworth wrote: "Thou hangest over the Infernal Pit/By one small threed,[1] and car'st thou not a whit." Jonathan Edwards had the same idea: "Sinners in the hands of an angry God," "Like spiders suspended over the mouth of Hell."

We must, however, look further than this if we would know the real Michael Wigglesworth. We must remember that he was a trained Greek and Latin scholar—one of the best that Harvard ever produced—and, in spite of the spiritual agonies of his early youth, an effective teacher. His use of the classics was utilitarian; it was kept strictly subordinate to Calvinistic

25

doctrines and at the same time serviceable for illustration of his Puritan message. Like many preachers in those days, he was a practicing physician.

We may turn to a later New Englander for assistance in the diagnosis of this complicated character. Emerson, the serene philosopher, makes two pertinent statements in his *Lecture on the Times*. The first reads: "There may be even truly great men, but with some defect in their composition which neutralizes their whole force." The second is: "What is noble will at first be defamed . . . but you who hold not of today, not of the times but of the Everlasting, are to stand for it; and the highest compliment man ever receives from Heaven is the sending to Him its disguised and discredited angels." Perhaps this fits Wigglesworth, "the little shadow of a man," with his profound classical scholarship, his Freudian worries, and his foggy concept of human relations, as he gradually but surely gained high standing in the Puritan community. In a modest letter to his old pupil Increase Mather he declined the Presidency of Harvard; and in 1697 he was elected a Fellow of the college, serving until his death in 1705.

Michael Wigglesworth was born at Hedon, near Hull, in Yorkshire, October 31, 1631; He was the son of Edward Wigglesworth, a fairly well-to-do tradesman. Yorkshiremen have always been forthright and definite in their views, and Edward was no exception. The condition of England in those days was perilous for anyone who called himself a Puritan and did not follow the orders of Laud and the High Church policy. Hence the Wigglesworths, with the large group of 1638, migrated to the Bay Colony, from an "ungodly place," with a son "not full seven years old," landing at Charlestown in August. Still on the move, they settled seven weeks later at Quinnipiac (New Haven). They were preceded by John Davenport and Theophilus Eaton, who put into satisfactory order matters both of church and state, on the strictest Puritan basis. They agreed "that church members only shall be free burgesses," thereby setting us to wonder, as Ezekiel Cheever did, whether the policy of these pioneers did not somewhat resemble the regime which they had left behind them in England. The living conditions of the migrants were notably poor; families were housed in underground cellars. In fact, it has been suggested that a flooded room in the winter season was responsible for much of Michael Wigglesworth's chronic illness. Those who survived subscribed to the Plantation Covenant and turned chaos into order. In all these adventures Edward Wigglesworth bore his part, though he was later afflicted with a crippling illness owing to overwork on his allotted acres.

At the age of eight, the young Wigglesworth was fortunate to come under the guidance of the great headmaster Ezekiel Cheever, with whom he studied until 1648.[2] This tutelage prepared him well for Harvard, where he welcomed educational advice from President Dunster and spiritual counsel from Thomas Shepard. It is clear that he profited much from these men of distinction and from his undergraduate tutor Jonathan Mitchell. High quality of mind, however, did not prevent Wigglesworth's beloved headmaster from getting into hot water over church regulations and disagreement with the elders of New Haven. Cheever felt and stated at a trial that religion had worked with too much domination over government and civilian life than was desirable in a balanced state. In 1650 he migrated back to the Bay. Ipswich, Charlestown, and the Boston Latin School had the benefit of his headmastership for eleven, nine and twenty-eight years respectively. Cheever received considerable and justifiable praise from Benjamin Tompson, Cotton Mather, and Samuel Sewall, which was more to him than any *monumentum aere perennius*. Cheever, his pupil Wigglesworth tells us, got him to "make Latin and to get forward apace," ready for Harvard after two and three-quarter years of schooling, and, most important, "to study with God and for God."

The academic record of young Wigglesworth was all that could be desired: he led his class at Harvard, resembling Jonathan Edwards, who was first at Yale and was also selected immediately as a college tutor. His position in 1652 was what we should now call a deanship of freshmen or a teaching fellowship. He made the most of the offerings in the college library, which was not limited to theological works. The routine of studies is familiar to all historians and educators: logic, Greek, Hebrew, physics, botany and history. There were many declamations and debates. Greek poets were turned into Latin; and Latin was to be spoken on all academic occasions. The textbooks were in Latin, and many of the authors had been read in school. We find Horace, Juvenal, Pliny, Persius, Plautus, Cicero, Homer, Hesiod, Theocritus, Aeschylus and Sophocles. Contemporary books such as Bacon's Essays and Peacham's *Garden of Rhetoric* were read extracurricularly. Romances often filled the students' commonplace books. It is interesting to note that one does not find arithmetic, geometry and astronomy on the schedule until the senior year. Aristotelian logic was gradually displaced by Ramean logic; it was Aristotle the political adviser, not the metaphysician, who influenced American thought during the Colonial period, and whose theories found their climax in the United States Constitution.

While Wigglesworth had not yet made up his mind to become a minister, and had toyed with the idea of a medical career, he took part in preaching "apprenticeship sermons," and had participated in academic discussions on various topics, studying the "doctrines, reasons, exhortations, and uses" which were an inheritance from Cicero and became the ingredients of Puritan and Presbyterian sermons. There were variations; but the standard *exordium, narratio, refutatio, probatio* and *peroratio*[3] served as models for presentation in court. This ground plan of viva voce discussion was especially appropriate for the New England Puritan, who throve on debate and argument. It trained him for the theological or the political arena. (Yale, for example, had at one time two classes of bachelor's degree, *ornatus ecclesiae* and *ornatus patriae*.)

Wigglesworth took his B.A. degree in 1651, having previously delivered an oration on *The Prayse of Eloquence,* recommending a combination of plain style and forceful presentation. He had been reading Demosthenes and Quintilian. His speech was an impressive indication of wide reading and keen analysis, of a much higher caliber than many of the *quaestiones* submitted for the advanced master's degree. Not content with this first oration, he produced in the same year a reflection of his interest in medicine, a short speech *De Microcosmo,* a commentary on the relation of the soul to the body. Upon graduation, he submitted a thesis on the necessity of a vacuum for all motions and activities of Nature entitled *Omnis natura inconstans est porosa.* Such were the emphatic and learned contributions of this delicate and sensitive young scholar who spent a large portion of his early life speculating on his sins and castigating his pride and his insufficient attention to the counsels of God. And yet his classical knowledge and his success as a teacher were clearly appreciated even by those who played mischievous tricks on him. There was no doubt of his high standards. In 1667 the Reverend Samuel Hooker wrote to Increase Mather,[4] a favorite pupil of Wigglesworth at Harvard, about the possibility of having his son study under Wigglesworth—"a man very *idoneus* [suitable] for such instruction as he needs."

In 1655 Wigglesworth married, and in the same year he accepted a call to the church at Malden, with which he was connected for the rest of his life, alternating between pulpit duties and intervals of illness. He had been offered an assistant-

ship at Hartford, which caused him some anxiety for he feared
that he had left the invitation dangling by not having replied.
"I knew not what God's will might be." "I was taken in some
falsity of speech on the Lord's Day." Was he playing off one
group against another? We find similar doubts and worries
about an offer from Salem, which he declined. Reading between the lines, it looks as if Mr. Stone of Hartford was
not enthusiastic about taking him into the Hartford Church.
In any case, he had plenty of invitations to be a guest preacher.[5]

For a curious mixture of religious devotion, self-castigation,
and a running account of his physical troubles, we may turn
to his diary, which covers the years 1653 to 1657. His naïve
frankness makes us feel almost hesitant to read the disclosures
of a frail physique, bodily ailments, and an easily wounded
spirit. He was close to God; but he found it difficult to face
human problems, which every dweller in the Bay had to
settle, with no blueprint to guide him except the Puritan code
of theological supremacy. Absurdly small matters weighed on
his soul, as did also the continual inroads of Arminianism or
Deism, and the Augustinian call to refer every situation to
the will of God.

A most impressive result of this self-communion is a sketch,
on September 15, 1655, of a pillar to which he gave the Biblical
title "Ebenezer" ("Hitherto the Lord hath holpen me"), "a
pillar to the prayer of his grace." He reflects on this symbol
in a passage compounded of Vergil and some of his own
"made Latin:"

> O Dulcis Memoria difficultatis praeteritae! Olim
> haec (quae nunc incumbunt mala, haec, inquam)
> meminisse iuvabit. Quae mala nunc affligunt,
> postea in laudem Dei nostramque voluptatem cedent.
> Quis triumphum caneret, quis spoliis onustus rediret
> victor, si numquam dimicaret?

(Sweet is the memory of bygone troubles! Some day it will be a pleasure to remember them, even those hardships, I repeat, which now press down upon me. The ills that now afflict me will yield to the glory of God, and to my own satisfaction. Who could sing a triumph song, who could return laden with trophies, if he never had to fight the battle?) This is more optimistic than most of the journal entries.

It is rare to find an out-and-out record of acknowledged success in this journal. One memorandum is noteworthy for its mixed emotion: "God hath prospered me this day in everything I set my hand unto . . . Blessed be his name . . . but I have no confidence in my doings: my soul longeth after God's grace." Sometimes God comes to the rescue in a matter of complicated difficulty. When he was detained at Concord by a knee-deep fall of snow, Wigglesworth "prayed, and God heard me and caused it to rain on Thursday and that night abated the snow to the ankles, thereby giving me a season of returning on Friday." On a journey to New Haven "God cleared away a fog." Academic ambition brings its dangers: "My proneness to satisfy my soul in my study's or pupils' progress, or anything without God, is the daily fear of my soul." "Too much bent of spirit to my studys and pupils, and affections dying towards God." The eternal conflict between prigs and saints repeats itself in the self-conscious Wigglesworth, who condemns his pride and confesses that he is apt to "run after mirth and recreation," Such relaxations are conspicuous by their absence. When his old friends at New Haven praised him and made much of him, he castigated himself for his pride in their welcome: "I was thereby led to over-ween my own worth."

The animal spirits of the Harvard students under his tutorship bothered him. We immediately think of the famous old "Tutor Flynt," and remember his way of handling rebellious youth. Wigglesworth's honored adviser Thomas Shepard, who had, to his own regret, wasted his opportunities as a Cambridge freshman at Emmanuel College, was more skillful in meeting the problem of flaming youth. Wigglesworth quoted him in the diary: "I tell you young persons that have passed your twenty years and slept out your opportunities, 'tis a wonder of wonders if ever God show you mercy." The pardonable desire of his pupils to avoid a course in Hebrew was defined by the tutor as "a spirit of unbridled licentiousness." "All my pains are fruitless for my pupils' spiritual good."

He had a disciplinary session with John Haynes, son of the Governor, who went off to Ipswich A.W.O.L., and then repeated the offense. The equivalent of jazz music in a student's room was to him sheer crime. "I am laden with a body of death." "An atheistic irreverent frame seizeth upon me." In the gloom of his meditations a brilliant phrase shines out: "Deliver me, our Lord, from a spirit of impenitent security!" Freudian self-consciousness and doctrinal doubts obsess him. "I was quite non-plus't about the Trinity." The well-known adage of Ovid[6] fitted his complaint: "I see the better, and I approve it; but I follow the worse." When he does well, he accuses himself of pride "because of secret joying in some conceived excellence in myself." Or: "I preached at Roxbury, the Lord assisting me more than formerly—O wretched worm that I am!" He did well in a disputation on Ramean logic; but pride manifested itself:[7] "Poor fool I!"

Two amusing dilemmas are recounted in his journal. While visiting the home of Jonathan Mitchell, Wigglesworth heard the stable door "beating to and fro with the wind." He was in some agony whether he should not have risen from bed and shut it himself. He was still more worried when "one that dwells in the house made light of it." Another failure to act involved a missing sword. Wigglesworth stated that he did not know the whereabouts of the weapon, when actually he knew who was keeping it. And a sample from the depths of absurdity: "I desire to hang down my head with shame before God. I neglected to speak to some whom I heard profanely laughing aloud. Lord forgive this neglect!" His conscience troubled him because he "transgressed the college law in speaking English" instead of the Latin required in academic communications.

The atmosphere of Harvard College must have been occasionally somber: "The Lord refused to hear my prayers for he [sic] whom in special I prayed for. I heard him in the forenoon with ill company playing music, though I had so solemnly warned him but yesterday of letting his spirit go after pleasures." Scattered through the journal are phrases from the Latin Vulgate and certain coined combinations, such as "Fons vitae me vivifica; Tu mihi principium; Tu mihi finis eris—My Alpha and my Omega." The latter quotation he borrowed from the first book of the Latin poet Propertius.

This pathetically humble and psychologically sensitive diary indicates that Wigglesworth was not destined to live as Shepard or Cotton—men who wrestled with the Angel and were forceful in community affairs. We are relieved to note that the diary came to an end in 1657. One cannot resist the temptation to say that here, as in Aristotle's definition of tragedy, was the purgation not so much of his eccentricities as of the morbidness and self-centered doubts which made his youth unwholesome and at times repellent. Let us see what happened to him in his latter years. We shall find a different person. It should always be remembered that Wigglesworth was fundamentally orthodox and in step with the Puritan idea. He was an able scholar, a well-equipped classicist; and as he grew more human and more mellow, his stature and his reputation increased.

His two books reflect his development from a recluse into a highly regarded spiritual and even practical leader in the life of the community. These are his *Day of Doom* (1662) and his *Meat out of the Eater* (1670). The contrast between the two volumes tells the story.

A preliminary vision which originated in 1659 laid the foundation for the *Day of Doom*:[8] "On the second day at night in my sleep I dreamed of the approach of the great and dreadful day of judgment, and was thereby exceedingly awakened in spirit (as I thought) to follow God with tears and cries until he gave me some hopes of his gracious good will toward me." The vision haunted him, and the next day he wrote: "I found myself unable to make any work of it at my studies, pride prevailing." Here was his opportunity, ready for one whose pen was qualified to tell the story and foretell the Great Occasion. Whatever we may think of its harshness, the book sold astonishingly well, and prompted Jonathan Mitchell, who had read the manuscript, to call it "the choicest food."

One hardly knows how to judge the *Day of Doom*. Was the writer "a morbid humorless selfish busy-body"[9] or, to use the Emersonian phrase, "a disguised angel"? The book is regarded as a typical New England production, but one thinks of many Colonial ministers, such as Charles Chauncy or Jonathan Mayhew, who were essentially human in their religious approach. Its latest editor[10] warns against forming an opinion by twentieth-century standards, for some sermons of John Donne, some pages of Edwards, and the "hell-roaring" of William Tennent are equally charged with explosive threats of eternal punishment. It may be only just to say that this gentle soul steeped himself in the horrors of extreme Calvinism in the hope that his readers would take pains to avoid the tortures of sinners. There is no classical serenity in this book; for the early Puritans had to struggle not only with pioneer hardships but also with the specific doctrine of saving souls by appeal to the Highest Power, almost on a competitive basis.

Today we feel a certain unanimity with the historian[11] who regards the writer as "attributing to the Divine Being a character the most execrable and loathsome to be met with, perhaps in any literature, Christian or Pagan." This was a pardonable overstatement, like that of Theodore Roosevelt, who called Tom Paine "a filthy little atheist;" but Wigglesworth himself felt that he was saving souls by such warnings.

Whether this masterpiece of what Dr. Johnson would have called "inspissated gloom" should be defined as poetry we may leave open to debate. It hardly deserves comparison with the works of Anne Bradstreet or Edward Taylor. At any rate, Wigglesworth knew what his readers wanted, and took pardonable pleasure in his success: "of 1800 copies there were scarcely any unsold," one for every twenty persons in New England.[12] It may be defined as in some ways revolting; but it was not heretical or radical.

As we select for typical portrayal a few stanzas, it bursts clearly upon us that Wigglesworth produced considerable doggerel, but that his sense of the dramatic was keen and of the first order. The scene is the throne of God: on the right the sheep, on the left the goats. The presiding judge, God, is a master of dialectic, subtle in his arguments and "divisions." The ringside seats, so to speak, are reserved for the real saints:

> Come, blessed ones, and sit on thrones,
> Judging the World with me!
> Come, and possess your happiness
> And bought felicitie.
> Henceforth no fears, no care, no tears
> No sin shall you annoy,
> Not anything that grief doth bring;
> Eternal Rest enjoy.

Next come the "unco guid," whose self-satisfaction causes them to fall short of these strict requirements. Those who died before they had a chance to reform were refused acceptance. Others vainly complained that God's word was "abstruse and harsh." There is no hope whatsoever for

> Ye sinful wights and cursed sprights
> That work iniquity ...
> Your portion take in yonder Lake
> Where Fire and Brimstone flameth.

A fortunate brother may look down from his throne at a condemned brother; and mothers are allowed no exemptions.

> The saints behold, with courage bold
> And thankful wonderment
> To see all those who were their foes
> Thus sent to punishment.

The decibel of denunciation, in a grand Wagnerian stanza, disposes of the wicked:

> With iron bands they bind their hands
> And cursed feet together,
> And cast them all, both great and small
> Into that lake forever.

As poetry, we can decide that while these verses, modeled on the old popular ballad form, are often mere jingle, they belong in a period which found them awesomely appropriate to meet the wiles of Satan, the Old Deluder.

Wigglesworth was an accomplished classicist who tossed off Latin tags and quotations, or coined semi-Latin phrases, but took care to keep his Latin strictly subservient to the Gospels. He regretted, or apologized for, his early absorption in heathen literature. Science and scholarship were regarded as useful but not of religious significance:

> Leave off your circles, Archimede, away:
> The King of Terrors calls, and will not stay.

In his "Prayer unto Christ," the proem to his *Day of Doom,* we have his viewpoint clearly stated:[13]

> I do much abominate
> To call the Muses to mine aid...
> Oh! What a deal of Blasphemy
> And Heathenish Impiety
> In Christian poets may be found,
> Where heathen gods with praise are crowned.
> They make Jehovah to stand by,
> Till Juno, Venus, Murcury, [sic]
> With frowning Mars and thundering Jove
> Rule Earth below and Heaven above.

His "Vanitie of Vanities" queries the value of earthly glories:

> If Wealth and Scepters could immortal make,
> Then, wealthy Croesus, wherefore art thou dead?
> If war-like force which makes the World to quake,
> Then why is Julius Caesar perishéd?
> Where are Scipio's Thunderbolts of war?
> Renowned Pompey, Caesar's Enemy?
> Stout Hannibal, Rome's Terror known afar?
> Great Alexander, what's become of thee?

Or, as an example to avoid:

> The Eastern Conqueror (Alexander) was said to weep
> When he the Indian Ocean did view,
> To see his conquest bounded by the Deep
> And no more worlds remaining to subdue.

Our life, Wigglesworth asserts, is summed up in the words of Pindar:[14]

> A dream, a lifeless picture, finely drest,
> A shadow of something, but naught indeed.

We find short vivid sayings: *amare Deum castigantem* ("Love thy God even when he chastens thee"). It is pardonable to forget the *Day of Doom,* but not the delicate little scholar who concluded this poem with a line reminiscent of St. Augustine: *Omnia praetereunt praeter amare Deum* ("all things pass away but the love of God").

Wigglesworth's *Meat out of the Eater,* which was published in 1670 and went through four editions within nineteen years, treats the candidates for sainthood more optimistically than does his *Day of Doom.*[15] Mercy is no less important than Justice. The title was suggested by the story of Samson: "out of weakness strength, out of strength sweetness." There are wider openings for salvation. Affliction can be turned into spiritual health. "God's blows were intended to save souls." Better a sick body and a well soul than vice versa. Cast yourself on the divine Mercy, and you need not fear. We may take one brief step into eternity and everlasting felicity.

The volume contains many illustrations taken from the classics and original Latin verses. The fourth "Song" begins with a Latin *consolatio*: "Solamen miseris socios habuisse doloris/ Christum cum Sanctis." (A consolation to sufferers in having Christ and the Saints as partners in sorrow.)

Meat out of the Eater deals with specific problems of the day, such as negro slavery. The symbolism of the debate between flesh and spirit is in the medieval tradition. There is a feeling of uplift. In the tenth "Song" the skies clear:

> Light, pardon, joy, and peace
> Eternal life and ease
> With full redemption
> Shall be thy portion.

There is more participation in current affairs, as in his earlier work *God's Controversy with New England* (published in 1662). Themes such as the drought, the epidemics, and the need for more spiritual living are touched upon. The poem opens with two stanzas in English, followed by a Latin quatrain to "Lector Amice;" the writer seems to be quite *en rapport* with his Malden congregation.

We are impressed by a beautifully constructed elegiac couplet:

> Christe, parum doleo quia te non diligo multum;
> Quodque parum doleo, causa doloris erit.

This the poet renders (in the tenth "Song"):

> Oh Christ, my grief is such
> Because I love not much,
> As added to my sore,
> Because I grieve not more.

Put more clearly, it might be: "Oh Christ, I suffer too little because I do not love thee enough; and the fact that I suffer too little, will be a cause of my suffering."

The second part of the book was "Riddles unriddled, or Christian paradoxes broke open, smelling of sweet spice." Crowder has summed up this change in Wigglesworth as he mastered his field and pleased his public. He moved from the *De Profundis* to a *Benedicite*.[16]

It is a pleasure to note the benevolent and affectionate relationships of this sensitive minister, as he drew towards his last year of 1705. We wish he could have known that his son Samuel would be the incumbent at Ipswich in 1714, that his younger son Edward would hold the Hollis Professorship of Divinity in Harvard College, that his grandson Edward and his great-grandson would follow in that same office. A parallel may be drawn here between the life of Wigglesworth and those of Edwards and Muhlenberg; we may leave it to be decided how much was due to heredity and how much to environment.

Allowing for all the thunder of the Judgment Day and the earlier obedience to a merciless creed, we are heartened to hear Wigglesworth's answer to one who asked for his views on the Salem episode, a still small voice contrasted with the whirlwind of the trials: "I fear that innocent blood has been shed . . . families of such as were condemned for supporting witchcraft have been ruined by taking away and making havoc of their estates . . . The whole country lies under a curse today." Still more emphatic was a similar remark: "I know it is a *noli me tangere* [a dangerous topic for discussion]; but lift up your voice like a trumpet!" Did he prompt Samuel Sewall to voice his confession in the Old South Church? The answer is not clear, but in any case he recommended to his old pupil Increase Mather that the Salem witchcraft problem was a public evil deserving legislation.

Despite a youth of physical and mental suffering, and a previously asocial attitude towards his work and his associates, Wigglesworth became a positive leader in the community. He delivered the Election Sermon at Cambridge in 1686 and in 1696 preached the annual sermon for the Ancient and Honorable Artillery, of which his friend Sewall was the Captain. He was comfortably at home in Malden, where his second wife made him an unselfish helpmate. His books had circulated well, and he spoke out on the secularism of the period.

The words of Emerson, quoted earlier, serve well to describe the life of this sensitive scholar-preacher. We may conclude from the earlier years of Michael Wigglesworth's life that the defects of gifted men often neutralize the effectiveness of their assets. Wigglesworth's success and fulfillment in later life, however, prove that one who holds fast to the Everlasting, even though once "a disguised and discredited angel," makes his way to Heaven and does honor to human kind.

IV

SAMUEL DAVIES

A Voice for Religious Freedom

THE SHORT LIFE of Samuel Davies, from 1723 to 1761, impresses us with the magnitude of his accomplishments. He was born at New Castle, in the "Lower Counties," now the State of Delaware, was educated at the famous Fagg's Manor School under Samuel Blair, and was graduated with highest distinction in the classical languages. He established a presbytery in Hanover, Virginia, and began a struggle for church independence which resulted later in the complete religious liberty and freedom from tithe-paying to the Episcopalian Church that Jefferson, with the aid of Madison, Mason, and George Wythe, secured after the Revolution. Elected President of the College of New Jersey (Princeton) in 1759, he spent two years in raising the standards and vitalizing the curriculum. Had he lived to a normal old age, he would have been another Witherspoon—statesman, churchman, and authoritative interpreter of the classical tradition. His travel diary reveals him comfortably at home with England and Scottish religious leaders; and his three volumes of sermons, replete with Greek and Roman illustrations "On the most Useful and Important Subjects," reward the reader to a greater extent than is usual with collected homilies.

We should remember that the Established Church of England was in the lifetime of Davies the official state religion. It was controlled by the Commissary at Williamsburg, who was responsible to the Bishop of London. There were plenty of dissenters of various denominations; but they were handicapped by a system which, though not overtly persecutional, was a barrier to independent organization. This took the form of refusal by the Established Church to grant preaching licenses to Presbyterian and other sects. Governor Gooch had allowed Davies to conduct services in Hanover County, but the Attorney General refused him a license to preach. Davies therefore devoted his European journey of 1752-1754 to securing this preaching privilege, which was eventually granted in England and Scotland. He was encouraged by Governor Dinwiddie, an alumnus of the University of Glasgow. There was no objection to the secular government of Virginia; and Davies distinguished himself as a patriotic British Colonial.

During the campaign for church independence, Samuel Davies seems to have been personally welcomed everywhere. To the Bishop of London he speaks out frankly: "If your lordship deal with us *secundum legem talionis* [an eye for an eye, or a fair reward for fair behavior], we expect favorable usage." He discusses the technique of New Testament phraseology with his clerical friends; whether, for example, in the volume called *The Tree of Life,* the word *Xylon* "has a plural signification." What are the shades of meaning in defining the Epithet *Poneros* (The Evil One)? He heartily approves the satire by John Witherspoon, at that time occupant of a Scotch parish, on *Ecclesiastical Characteristics*—a vigorous attack against the Moderates or Deists who had the effrontery to place Aristotle, Seneca, and other "good Pagans" on a level with scriptural authority, following the erroneous views of Shaftesbury and Francis Hutcheson. He is amused by a row of portraits in the study of Dr. Watts the hymn-writer, and a vacant place next to them marked, according to Horace, "Est locus pluribus umbris" (There is room for some humble hangers-on), and a Latin query of the Doctor's expressing the hope that he may ultimately join this great gallery: "Quis me doctorum propria dignabitur umbra?" This exhibit entertains him; but he is somewhat shocked when he notes that the distinguished Dr. Doddridge has placed the pseudo-Epicurean motto "Dum vivimus, vivamus" under his own picture. He did not himself regard Petronius as a model. But he was glad to see over one door the sentiment "Doctrinae Filia Virtus" (Virtue is the daughter of Learning) and the Horatian corollary over the other door: "Filia Matre Pulchrior." With all these dignitaries Davies held his own.

Throughout his travels in Britain he carried with him the haunting sense of sin which is always distinctive in his writings—"Caelum, non animum, mutant qui trans mare currunt" (Men who fare overseas may change their climate but never their souls).[1] In his diary he comments on the Vergilian *auri Sacra fames* (the cursed craving for gold), and echoes Horace in his longing for home, with *animae dimidium meae,* (Thou who art half my soul)—a tribute to his absent wife.

Davies was at his best in his sermons—"a man," as a colleague said of him, "of uncommon furniture, both of gifts and grace." We are struck by the clarity of the addresses, but cannot help being puzzled about the capacity of the Hanover County audiences to assimilate his learning. Most of the sermons we are concerned with antedate his Princeton incumbency. Probably they were specially prepared for publication. It is obvious that the Presbyterians were interested in a good education, and welcomed such stylistic touches as the readers of Sam Adams found in his articles in the *Boston Gazette*. Typical of Adams's subject matter were "Old Romans," "A Christian Sparta," and an article on the doings of the tribunes. Davies holds the same views as Roger Williams, believing that the martyrdoms in the early Empire made Christianity flourish, while the official adoption thereof by Constantine and a state religion led to heresies, greed, superstition, and bureaucracy. Whenever he can consistently do so, Davies supplies a historical event as confirmation of his scriptural statements. In his sermon on *The Mediatorial Kingdom,* alluding to the prophecy of a Messiah in Judah, he calls to mind a passage from the *Histories* of Tacitus, and another from the *Vespasian* of Suetonius:[2] "Percrebruerat Oriente toto vetus et constans opinio esse in fatis ut eo tempore Judea profecti rerum potirentur." (There had spread all over the Orient an old and established belief, that it was fated at that time for men coming from Judea to rule the world.) This rumor of possible future domination by the Jews doubtless had much to do with the Roman destruction of Jerusalem.

It is fair to say that at a critical stage in colonial history the theological problems of Davies did not interfere with his patriotism. The situation was eased by the need of good soldiers as volunteers for the French and Indian Wars, especially after the Braddock tragedy. Davies warmly supported Colonel Washington. His recruiting sermon of May 8, 1758, is characteristic both of the Scotch-Irish or Welsh fighting qualities and of the delicate balance which the clergy were supposed to maintain between the classics in which they were steeped and the revealed religion which they professed: "Oh for all-pervading force of Demosthenes' oratory—but I recall my wish, that I may correct it—oh for the influence of the Lord of armies, the God of battles, the Author of true courage!" But at the most discouraging period of the war he called for courageous resistance, invoking the famous ode of Horace which dealt with the Roman surrender and the heroic self-sacrifice of Regulus: "Proh Curia! Inversique mores" (Shame on our government and our weakened morale!).[3]

It is natural that, no matter how highly trained a scholar

he might have been, the Hanover preacher would let nothing stand in the way of revealed religion. There was no compromise in his Princeton *quaestio* of 1753, when he received his Master's Degree: *Personales Distinctiones in Trinitate sunt Aeternae.* As did Edwards and Witherspoon, he declared that "a man of common sense, with the assistance of Sacred Scriptures, can form a better system of religion and morality than the wisest philosopher. . . . In the Kingdom of Heaven, any common Christian is greater than all the Socrateses, the Platos, the Ciceros, and the Senecas of antiquity." "True faith is better than the heathen philosophers; for though there were many good things in them, yet who gave authority to Socrates, Plato or Seneca to assume the province of lawgivers, and prescribe to men's consciences?" In his *Rule of Equity* sermon he wrote: "Were I reading to you a letter of moral philosophy in the school of Socrates or Seneca, what I have offered might be sufficient." But much more than this is necessary—Divine authority and the Master's service.

Dante's dwellers in Limbo after all are equally unhelpful on the subject of immortality. "The Socrateses, the Platos, and the Ciceros of Greece and Rome, after all their searches, were more perplexed on this point than a plain common Christian." The Pagans "indulged in chimerical premises—transmigration of souls, pre-existence of souls, *Anima Mundi,* etc." As Davies realized, even Socrates has doubts whether death means annihilation or transfer elsewhere. There is the same denunciation of sinners that we find in Jonathan Edwards; Davies actually uses the figure of the condemned soul and the spider held over the flame. In his sermon on *The General Resurrection,* the dead come to life. Their limbs may be scattered: "here the head and there the trunk, and the ocean rolling between"; but they are joined together in the original body to appear before the Judgment Seat. At this point the preacher could not resist a classical comparison: "This was the fate of Pompey—his body was left on the African shore and his head carried over the Mediterranean to Julius Caesar."

There is, in fact, a progressively increasing use by Davies of Greco-Roman illustrations, subordinated to the Christian message. The Supreme Good of the ancient philosophers is described as the perfect condition of the believer's soul. The *divinae particula aurae*[4] of Horace, the spirit, is immortal. Saint Paul, on Mars' Hill at Athens, introducing his address by a line from Aratus and the altar to an Unknown God, excuses the Athenian ignorance of the true faith but ends by "exposing their superstitions and calling them off from their idols to the worship of One God." Paul before his conversion "kicked against the gods"; but, as Davies remarks, so did many others, rebuked by Pindar, Euripides, and Terence.[5] Spiritual pride should be corrected: "Why need there be so many religious Thrasos?" The absolute allegiance implied in the Lord's Supper is mentioned by St. Augustine and fortified by Horace with his soldier's oath: "Non ego perfidum dixi sacramentum.[6] In illustration of Christ's martyrdom, commanded by God, we have the story of Brutus and the execution of his two sons as a matter of duty and obedience to law. The sources of these classical echoes are not always direct; some are from a well-stocked memory and others from florilegia, as "Universal History, vol. XI, p. 360."

Religion the highest Wisdom and Sin the greatest Folly refers to the use by Pythagoras of *Philosophos* (lover of wisdom) and the sage's feeling that *sophos* alone was "too ostentatious and arrogant." *Practical Atheism Exposed* was a sermon preached both in Hanover and at Princeton. Here the two classical authors whom Davies regards most highly are invoked to uphold the existence of a Divine Providence. Plato (via Gale's *Philosophia Generalis*) is certain that there is such a Providence. Cicero, in his *De natura deorum,* agrees:

"If the Gods neither are able nor willing to help us, why do we pray to them?"[7] Four other passages in Cicero are cited to prove "Dominos esse omnium Deos." Plato preserves the climax of testimony from his *Euthyphro:* "Holiness preserves our houses and public communities"; conversely, Epicurus the Atheist "sustulit omnem funditus religionem"[8] (did away with all religion, root and branch). A God exists "by the light of Nature"; the heathen "had all of them *Gentilial* gods for the protection of the Nation," as Mars and Minerva. With such faith, the good man, after death, will possess a "plerophory of joy."

On *Miracles and Portents* the Virginia preacher maintains the traditional view that these manifestations are signs of divine approval or disapproval. The French and Indian war scare was a tragic source of anxiety; and a sermon by Davies entitled *Signs of the Times* is replete with instances from Greek and Roman history.[9] Earthquakes, pestilences, comets, a blood-red sky, the Tiber flowing backwards, the sacred chickens who refused to eat, and the final recourse to the Sibylline Books—all these are recorded, especially from the *Naturales quaestiones* of Seneca, Cicero's *De divinatione,* or his *De natura deorum.* Homer, Hesiod, Vergil, Horace, the Elder Pliny, Tacitus, Suetonius, and Plutarch appear as proof of all these inflictions, which are naturally channelled into warnings of suffering or sudden death—only surmountable by true Christians. In this particular sermon, with an astonishing power of memory, Davies brings the world of the ancients into Hanover County.

Conscience and sin find approved parallels: "Even the heathen poet Juvenal,[10] not famous for the delicacy of his morals, could speak feelingly of its secret blows, and of agonizing sweats under its tortures": *Frigida mens est/ Criminibus, tacita sudant praecordia culpa"*—"His soul is cold with crime; he sweats with the secret consciousness of sin." The sinner is faced with "everlasting chains of darkness." This Calvinistic touch is elaborated by a passage from Vergil's terrors of Tartarus:[11]

> Non mihi si linguae centum sint oraque centum,
> Ferrea vox, omnes scelerum comprendere formas,
> Omnia poenarum percurrere nomina possim.

("No; had I even a hundred tongues, and a hundred mouths, and lungs of iron, not then could I embrace all the types of crime, or rehearse the whole muster-roll of Vengeance," in Conington's translation.)

The world is a transitory pageant: Lucian is called upon as witness, from *Dialogue,* xxxii, "Murphy's edition." The only remedy is to keep one's eyes fixed on heavenly things, trusting, as Horace says,[12] in the eye rather than the ear:

> Segnius irritant animos demissa per aurem
> Quam quae sunt oculis subjecta fidelibus.

(Our minds are less vividly stirred by what we absorb through the ear, than by exposure to the truthful eye.) Christianity should be a *vision* as well as a message. This is a motto frequent in Colonial literature; Increase Mather uses it as introductory to his account of King Philip's War.

The good Christian aims to be as much like his Master as possible. Davies seeks to illustrate this point in the words of Plutarch:[13] "After attacking a precipitous citadel, he [Alexander] was urging on the young Macedonians, and addressing one who bore the name of Alexander, said: 'It behooves thee at least to be a brave man, even for thy name's sake.' When the young man, fighting gloriously, fell, the king was pained beyond measure."

On the death of King George the famous dictum of Horace, used by Wise and Sewall and many others on the same occasion, was recalled aptly by Davies: "Death intrudes into palaces as well as cottages, and arrests the monarch as well as the slave." So did the prophecy of future glory for the new king, taken from the fourth Eclogue of Vergil and the prospect of a happy reign. These offhand allusions are so frequent that we may close the list at this point, with the Senecan warning to the ambitious person who is "standing not merely on the edge of a precipice but also on slippery ground." [14]

Unlike most of the Colonial clergy in the northern regions, Davies has no complaint about the so-called "mixed government" which many others felt might be improved.[15] Even the appointment of an Episcopalian bishop would do no harm, provided that he be "an apostolic New Testament bishop," like the presbyter in the Scriptures. Davies asks only that the Presbyterians and other dissenters have their own religious freedom.

One comes to the conclusion that this minister of the Gospel, highly regarded in his own day and deserving of more attention now, made a wise use of his classical material. This was appropriate in an era when the Greco-Roman tradition was at its peak, and when the common-sense philosophy had spread through the Middle Colonies. Samuel Davies is entitled to an honored place among the leaders of the church, with those New Englanders who refused to let learning lie buried in the dust. Davies, physically frail but spiritually forceful, died too soon; but he undoubtedly broke ground for the state law of spiritual liberty in which Jefferson deservedly took such pride.

V

HENRY MELCHIOR MUHLENBERG

A Spiritual Trouble-shooter

WHEN HENRY MUHLENBERG was appointed by the Hanover Consistory in Germany, and empowered to reorganize the Lutheran churches of Pennsylvania and of the neighboring provinces, he justified the choice by forty-five years of earnest and successful labor. This spiritual trouble-shooter[1] won the respect of the German, English, Dutch, Swedish, and Scottish settlers who made up the cosmopolitan population of the province. With his classical university training, his broad interpretation of theology, his tact in dealing with other denominations, and his surmounting of physical hardships under pioneer conditions, he deserves the attention he has not adequately received as a self-forgetting comforter of souls and an organizer of the highest quality. The individual was as important to him as the congregation. A friend of his youth prophesied that his character, with his "bull-necked" power of resistance to difficulties and his persistent search for the ideal, would carry him through in triumph. "Our hoard was little but our hearts were great."

The keen desire for learning characteristic of many Germans in those days revealed itself in Muhlenberg's youth. Henry Muhlenberg was born on September 6, 1711, at Einbeck in the principality of Hanover, the son of a shoemaker who was also a deacon and a town councillor. His mother was the daughter of an army officer. Their religion was Lutheran and their politics were strongly British-Hanoverian. They followed the Augsburg Confession—to which Henry adhered throughout his life. The young Muhlenberg attended a good, local classical school from an early age; his Latin was so thoroughly mastered that he was comfortably at home in that language, both written and oral. He studied the organ and gave lessons on the clavichord. That his musical accomplishments were not superficial is proved by the fact that later, in Philadelphia, the virtuoso and composer Francis Hopkinson consulted him with regard to the playing of these instruments and the details of their construction. A short stretch of apprentice teaching at home, in the orphan schools at Zellerfeld, and in the Harz mountains in the Baroness von Gersdorf's institute at Groshennersdorf, preceded his entry into Göttingen in 1735; he then proceded to Halle. In 1739 he was ordained at Leipzig.

Even in his early years, at home in Hanover, Muhlenberg found his work complicated by local jealousies. His opponents called him a "Pietist," a word which from the historian's viewpoint would be no insult. Some held that he was "an itinerant fanatic." There is no doubt that he was "itinerant" in the best sense of the word, for he earned in Pennsylvania the title of "The Saddle-Bag Preacher." [2] Like John Wesley, he almost lived on horseback. Others accused him of being "given to conventicles." He debated these and other issues with the consistory at Hanover, and was in demand for his sermons, as was also Michael Wigglesworth even before he received his master's degree at Harvard.

The Burgomaster sometimes argued with Muhlenberg in open meeting; both contestants used Latin terminology, and Muhlenberg stumped his critic by asking him to decide whether the point at issue was to be interpreted "Juridicé, Politicé,

Philosophicé, or Theologicé." These technical terms go back to Roman oratory, and (with the exception of Theologicé) were discussed at length by Quintilian.[3]

This argumentative practice stood him in good stead in the wilder American scene to which he was called. We note him later talking with the chief justice of Georgia in Latin, discussing "Leibnitzian, Aristotelian, and Wolffian philosophy." With the captain of the Georgia Packet he conversed in Latin, checking his pronunciation and improving his speaking knowledge of English. Before crossing the Atlantic, he reported to the Reverend Frederick Michael Ziegenhagen, the Lutheran Court Preacher to King George II in London, and began a friendship which was maintained for many years. Henry preached in some non-Lutheran churches and took his turn at services in the Court Chapel. His certificate, given him by Ziegenhagen and endorsed by Count Reuss and Augustus Francke, was greeted with approval in America, except by a few disgruntled parsons who mixed politics with routine religion and whose parishes needed a spiritual house-cleaning. It is significant that in Philadelphia Dr. Peters of the Established Church of England and Pastor Wrangel of the Swedish congregation exchanged pulpits with Muhlenberg and cooperated in every way. We also note his continuing harmonious relationship with the great popular preacher George Whitefield, a graduate of Pembroke College, Oxford, whom he regarded as a superlative advocate of revealed Christianity.

Muhlenberg came, from a thorough classical university system in Germany, to a province which was no enemy to higher learning and the Greco-Roman tradition, both for the laymen and clergy.[4] William Penn had studied and published tracts on the comparison of the Inner Light of the Quakers with the testimony of the pre-Socratic philosophers. He pointed to the Daimon of Socrates as an illustration of the Eternal Word and the Logos. As a Christ Church student he had read of the "Genius, Angel, or Guide." Francis Daniel Pastorius could stand alongside any provincial for linguistic knowledge; he was comfortably at home in seven languages. Kelpius, the Hermit of Germantown, had learned Latin, Hebrew, Greek, English, and German. Peter Miller, a member of the American Philosophical Society, was a Heidelberg graduate; his establishment at Ephrata was a center of classical scholarship. There were experts in Latin hymnology and Oriental languages. The mere name of James Logan suggests mastery of Greek and Latin. Small wonder, then, that Henry Muhlenberg desired improved standards of education for the Lutheran ministry. He asked for a thorough experience of study and learning from his candidates. We read in his journal for June 16, 1750,[5] "We laid before Mr. Weygand [an applicant for ordination] the Latin examinations which he was to answer . . . and afterwards I delivered a brief Latin address to my colleagues." Even in the forest parishes a college or university degree was most desirable.

Besides offering an open door to learning, Penn's policy of free church and free speech opened the way for controversies on all sorts of subjects,[6] expressed in broad-sides and pamphlets. There appeared "The Lives and characters of Sejanus and Protesilaus and many other noted politicians," "The Conspiracy of Catiline," quotations from Juvenal the satirist, and a pastoral poem by "Agricola" entitled "The Squabble." In 1767 there was published an essay *On True Happiness,* (subtitled *the Character of Eusebius*) and a letter from "Atticus" to his friend Bradford. Amid a welter of almanac satire, we note an abusive skit by the Tory father of Leigh Hunt: "Dialogue number 8 between the giant Polyphemus and his son Jack Nothing—an exercise had this morning in Scurrility Hall." Headmaster John Beveridge was pouring out Latin verses— *Epistulae Familiares.* Muhlenberg wisely kept out of range of this sarcastic artillery, but he took the American part in the Stamp Act, writing in German on the patriot side and enduring some criticism because of his peaceful policy.

Muhlenberg's main task was to help in the education of his

provincial congregation. The university program to which we have referred acted as a contribution towards this end. The church in Germany being an *ecclesia plantata* (an established body), the church in Pennsylvania was an *ecclesia plantanda,* or *colligenda* (a church still to be established) with similar principles and doctrines. Muhlenberg believed that a classical training, with the essence of theological fundamentals, was the proper base. This was as important for the frontier as it was for Halle.

The Congregational Constitution which Muhlenberg worked to establish from 1748 onwards was definitely accepted on October 18, 1762; he was elected *Praeses* of the Evangelical Lutheran Ministerium of Pennsylvania. He had thus carried out the plan conceived by the authorities across the ocean, but along broad lines and in his own way. His efforts were crowned in his old age by the editorship in 1786 of his *Erbauliche Lieder-Sammlung,* a collection of hymns for which he wrote the preface, insisting on the inclusion of "the ancient medieval hymns which have been familiar to all Lutherans and cannot be left out." He rejected certain pieces which he regarded as too infantile or too reminiscent of the sensual passages in the Song of Solomon. The old man who died on October 7, 1787, aged seventy-six, exercised his habit of constructive criticism up to the very end.

Muhlenberg looked upon the classics as underlying training for mastery of theology and church procedure. He schooled himself to preach in Latin, English, Dutch, and of course, German. The aesthetic or cultural side did not interest him as much as the practical. He admitted the superiority of the Moravians in their educational system, although he quarreled over doctrinal matters with Count Zinzendorf. He agreed that the schooling conducted by the Germans at Nazareth, especially in Latin and music, was of a high quality.[7] He also admired the thorough classical and theological training offered by the Presbyterians at the Log College and subsequently at Princeton. He declared that the Lutherans "needed a seminarium"; and a careful reader of his journals notes a prejudice, sometimes hinted and not always broad-minded, against the highly organized and widely traveled Moravians.

Two interesting interviews which he records illustrate his fundamental knowledge of the relationship between learning and religion. One of them is described as follows: "In the evening I had a visit from a scholar from New England,[8] Mr. Webster, who was desirous of speaking with me concerning the doctrine and discipline of the Lutheran Church . . . I answered his questions concerning our doctrine of Baptism, the Lord's Supper, Predestination, Divine Providence . . . I asked him whether and when God had begun his work of grace, repentance, and conversion in him. He gave a good account thereof and finally asked me to read some Latin and Greek to him, because he wanted to hear my pronunciation and accentuation, etc." Muhlenberg answered him just as far as he was pressed for helpful information.

The second experience involved deeper discussion. On a visit to Heidelberg, in Berks County, after his delivery of a sermon, Muhlenberg wrote: "I met a school master who far surpassed us in learning and experience. He had gathered quite a store of the polemical theological writings of the last century which abound in Latin phrases and words, and he requested me to explain such as he had noted down in a catalog which he had with him. I replied that we possess the Saving Word of God in the Holy Bible, pure and clear in our mother tongue, and that we can attain to life and light in the order of repentance and faith without Latin scraps . . . We have also been blest in this century by many edifying works in our mother tongue . . . We tried to refer him to his own heart and to the primary roots of true conversion and change of outlook. But he had already experienced all that we could tell him, and more besides. He said that he lacked only this one thing—that he might understand the Latin words *Festum Nativitatis, Circumcisionis, Epiphaniae, Resurrectionis, Trinitatis, Dominicae Ascensionis, Pentecostis* . . . he had long harbored a secret desire to be a minister and for this purpose had purchased at great cost the famous Erdman Uhsen's *Redner mit Oratorischen Kunstgriffen*.[9] We urged him to begin by learning to experience what Christ prescribed in Matthew, chapter 5, concerning poverty of spirit, mourning, purity of heart, hunger and thirst, etc.; but he stuck to me like a burr on a coat, and would not rest until I had *revealed to him the Latin Mysteries*. Then he bade us farewell with a relieved conscience and left us, tired out, to ourselves."

On another occasion, when he was asked by Dr. Pemberton, the New York Presbyterian, why the Lutherans did not use the Roman Stoic stages of *cognitio, assensus,* and *fiducia,* in their definitions of progressive conversion, Muhlenberg simply referred him to the Confession of the Lutheran church. All these answers indicate that this highly trained theologian and scholar, a product of the classical and logical program of the German universities, exhibited his learning very sparingly in his career as a Pennsylvania missionary. His Greek and Latin were a fundamental part of his educational background, and he was thoroughly satisfied with them as a necessary element in his studies. But his use of them was brief and to the point, not overloaded with technicalities. It was his answer to many questions, theological, physical, or legal. He spoke of *species facti, cum Judicio et Grano salis, Preserva te ipsum, dicta probantia, Actus Promotionis* (Commencement exercises), *per fas et nefas* (rightly or wrongly), *opus operatum* (a review of the facts). He liked the Latin equivalent. Horace's *Risum teneatis* was invoked on the absurdities of the Pennsylvania state constitution of 1776: "You can't help laughing at it." [10] In describing the prevalent disease of pleurisy, he turned to

the classics, with symptoms as technical as a doctor's pre-
scription. Even seasickness was lamented in Latin: "Inversus
motus peristalticus!"

He congratulated the Salzburgers in Georgia: they had done
so well that no one could call them an *ecclesia oppressa*.
Much of his letter writing was done in Latin; and he followed
Luther in holding that *"oratio, meditatio,* and *tentatio"* would
make a theologian. When his son Peter showed him a poem
that he composed for a friend's wedding, he advised against
sending it: "I found that he had the gift of rhyming but
not of poetry. I kept the verses back, *triti proverbii haud
immemor: si tacuisses, philosophus mansisses:* I thought of
the well-worn proverb 'If you had kept silent, you might
have remained a philosopher.'" In his old age, he called
himself a *pondus inutile terrae.* He believed that in reading
the signs of the times one should view realistically the *regnum
politicum et ecclesiasticum.*

Muhlenberg sketched his own duties with a quotation from
one of his Hanoverian friends: "The sainted Count Reuss
once said 'Our Lord Jesus, the head Shepherd, needs not only
under-shepherds, but also sheep dogs who must round up the
sheep and goats in the pasture by barking at them and herding
them into one flock.'"[11] This is the metaphor used by the
poet Edward Taylor of Massachusetts, who described, in a
passage reminiscent of the Greek poet Theocritus, the duties
of the sheep dog, barking at the strayed animals and preserving the flocks from harm. Taylor's language, with a slight
alteration, indicates that Satan could be used as one who
scares the sheep into their proper place by his threats. For
persons like Taylor and Muhlenberg, Satan was an important
factor in the process of conversion: you must hate him or
fear him as a bad example. So the Devil can be useful also
as a deterrent: "Whose barking is to make thee cling/ Close
underneath thy Savior's wing." Our conscientious Lutheran

would doubtless have believed that he himself should be the sheep dog rather than that Satan should be relied on as a warning to the faithful. Under certain circumstances Satan could be Mephistopheles.

We find in Muhlenberg's journals some brief epigrams and phrases based on classical origins. For example, during an "edifying conversation" at the home of Jacob Duché (who opened the Continental Congress with prayer and later turned Tory) Muhlenberg summed up the essence of revealed religion as "the working of God's spirit upon the soul," and called it in Latin the *Principium cognoscendi.* Commenting upon the worldly habits of fellow citizens, he advised them on what the Stoics entitled *adiaphora* ("indifferent"), the tastes and normal activities which, in moderation, are permissible. These are social relations, desirable recreation and hobbies, according to the interests of the individual. He condemned abuses in dancing, the theatre, frivolity, and carelessness in balancing income with expenditure. He criticized a young clergyman (who was later dismissed from his position) for such faults: he might, according to his advisor, "have become a real *theologus* if he had been in earnest about his own soul and the souls of others." Under the proper circumstances his *adminicles* (or supporting documents) and theological works would have afforded some moral guidance. These "matters of indifference" were important but not to be classified on the same basis as spiritual obligations. Muhlenberg revealed an extreme strictness towards worldly honors when his son Ernest and his son-in-law Kuntze received honorary degrees from the University of Pennsylvania. He queried in his Journal: "What good is *onomatopoeia* for the kingdom of Jesus Christ?"

There are many incidental references to the classics in Muhlenberg's writings. For oratory the essence is *non multa sed multum.* In a letter to a Danish officer Henry emphasized the importance of a plain style—Cicero's Attic rather than the full-blown Asianic, free from metaphysical complications. During the critical war days, when the stout-hearted old Lutheran was unpopular because of his refusal to take an active part, he noted that "certain persons call me a traitor and lay the blame on *causae secondariae.*" Physicians are entitled "Aesculapii." Regarding the balloon experiments of 1784, "Daedali will be making waxen wings and, like Phaethon, will want to rule the sun." The command to love one's neighbor goes far beyond the *sensus litterae.* In a letter to Franklin he uses the rare word "perturbate" for "disturb" or "upset." When accused of being a Tory, he regarded such rumors as "foul vapors from the Father of Lies let loose and spread *methodo mathematica.*" When he was serving as one of the arbitrators in a divorce case, the petitioner submitted his reasons, "couched in Ciceronian Latin, *methodo demonstrativa.*" In the horrors of war, "if the temples should burn along with other things, Vespasian will say: 'We have no need of priests.'" To a German who asked why Lutheran ministers instigate war, he remarked: "The Emperor set fire to Rome and blamed the Christians for it."

He referred to selfish old bachelors who have "revolved around their own axis and *aeolipile.*" This rare word is recorded in the Oxford Dictionary as "an instrument for showing forces of steam escaping through a narrow aperture"; and we note its connection with the mythological figure of Aeolus, God of the winds. And was he thinking in terms of the ancient metrical marching anapaests when he heard the thunder of the Brandywine cannon and watched the troops marching past his home? "What one used to hear in the country at this season of the year was the music of the swish of flails in three-quarter time . . . and now, drums, fifes, and war-cries." All this confusion he endured, and amid his complaints noted that "the New England troops have a good reputation: they do not curse and swear like others, nor do they rob and steal."

On May 7, 1778 a puzzling entry is found in Muhlenberg's

notebook: "Yesterday, in the American army, they marched three times around a bonfire." Was this a postponed May Day performance, mere coincidence, or something symbolic? Was it to celebrate the evacuation of Philadelphia by the British? Or to lament the death of some well-known officer? We are reminded of the pyre and the marchers at the funeral of Achilles, or the passage descriptive of the ceremonies in memory of Beowulf: "Then about that barrow the battle-keen rode, Atheling-born, a band of twelve, Lament to make, to mourn their King, Chant their dirge, and their Chieftan honor." [12]

Muhlenberg handled matters of inter-church relationships skillfully. When a Dutch and German group of Lutherans reported that an Anglican church was to be built in their neighborhood and they had been offered facilities there for their own services if they would raise part of the cost, Muhlenberg commented that such *Dubia Vexata* were difficult to settle, and that the home universities with their expert knowledge were too far away for a *responsum*: "When a *collegium polemico-disputatorium* takes place in academic surroundings, one side always wins; but it is not easy when one has to confront the authors of such a plan face to face." A learned university professor in Europe could get at the root of the *status controversiae* and deal with abstractions. "But when one takes it in the concrete, it would probably be difficult to debate with the Pope in Rome." In a faraway colony such problems cannot be as learnedly solved as in the halls of Göttingen or Jena or Halle. Civil and theological headquarters were too far distant.

At any rate he could handle the agenda of a local synod and keep bravely on with his rides over rough trails to preach a sermon or conduct a christening: "I must seek out the sheep, develop a Westphalian stomach to digest hard fare, and be equipped with a great soul and with love towards Christ and his lost sheep; for this is an *ecclesia colligenda,* depending

on our drawing worshippers into the fold." He kept aloof
on principle from the complicated politics of the province.
The *vox populi* could easily become the *vox diaboli*. In a letter
to one of his daughters he cautioned her *maritus dilectissimus*
to be careful in his communications: he might risk "lighting
upon Scylla in order to avoid Charybdis." Ministers should
not be civil judges or arbitrators: the government has nothing
to do with religious matters. "A preacher must fight his way
through, with the sword of the Spirit alone." [13] He coined
a phrase, *Providentia Specialissima*—a reliance on God's assistance in times of doubt and danger.

The human touch was uppermost in all Muhlenberg's dealings. He was at home in the Royal Chapel of King George,
and also among the Indians. The latter nicknamed him "Gach-
swongarorachs," which meant "a saw for woodcutting," referring to his skill in "cutting hard, knotty, intractable hearts
and transforming them into something useful." Like James
Logan, who entertained the Indians at his country place, or
like William Byrd who made companions of the good Indians
over the campfires, Muhlenberg describes their superstitions
and follows William Penn's method in recognizing their rights.
He humorously remarked that their folklore could supply
material for a Latin college master's or doctor's dissertation.
(When a friend commented on a possible Roman-like augury
for the significance of some ravens and crows fighting, Muhlenberg remembered the ancient passage in Livy but maintained
that this was no parallel). Muhlenberg and his father-in-law
Conrad Weiser agreed that it would improve the settlers in
their relations with the Indians if, instead of forced acceptance
of the white men's ways, they would study their customs,
language, and "police," translating our truths into their *mores,*
and even "learning their melodies and tones—and then with
God's blessing await the fruitage." William Bartram, the botan-
ist-explorer, made a similar suggestion regarding the treatment

of his Seminole and Creek friends when he lived among them happily some forty years later.[14]

Muhlenberg had to endure some denunciation at the beginning of the Revolution; but his three sons, who were all ordained ministers, "turned professional" in war, politics and education. They brought him round to a serious conception of the future United States. He read Paine's *Common Sense* in a German translation and admitted to his son-in-law Schultze that the Americans were right. His son Peter ("Teufel Piet") had been ordained by an Anglican bishop; his other sons Frederick and Ernest were consecrated in October 1770 as *Collaboratores Ministerii,* with the usual extensive reading in classics, logic and theology. They were examined in Latin and German. Ernest had studied the Greek New Testament, Herodotus, Thucydides, Homer, Callimachus, and in Latin, Eutropius, Nepos, Terence, Caesar, Cicero, Livy, Ovid, Vergil, and Horace. Their father questioned their interest in politics: he wrote with regret "Having learned with dismay that *vox populi per plurima vota* has elected my son Frederick Augustus a member of the state government and that the Assembly had even chosen him chairman after two years in Congress." But he finally gave them his blessing, and a benediction to Washington on his Farewell Address to Congress: "How rare are such true professions in the present generation of this so-called great world!" Before their final decisions the brothers baited each other in macaronic German, English, and Latin letters. When Ernest received an honorary degree from the University of Pennsylvania, his brother Frederick sent him a burlesque poem of congratulation, in Latin, with hexameters and caricatures of ancient authors. But they were all dedicated to large-scale public service—a general, a statesman, and a college president who was a botanist of international reputation. Benjamin Rush, a discriminating commentator, praised Ernest, the head of Franklin College (now Franklin and Marshall): "His

extensive knowledge and taste in the arts and sciences, joined
with his industry in the discharge of the duties of his station,
have afforded to the friends of learning in Pennsylvania the
most flattering prospects of the future importance and useful-
ness of this institution." [15]

Their father's death on October 7, 1787, seems to have been
a call to many of his family to carry on the tradition of
contributing generously to local and national welfare.[16] How
much was hereditary and how much environmental is a matter
for speculation. They were all believers in the New America,
and actors in its progress. They were all steeped in the classics
and stout supporters of a university training. They inherited
from their father a willpower to face and conquer difficulties.
His successful efforts in bringing about Lutheran unity illustrate the one quality. His endurance of hardships speaks for
itself. "Crossing the ice-bound Perkiomen Creek, my horse
floundered and stuck fast. I went ahead to break the ice.
My companion followed in the footsteps which my horse
had broken . . . I arrived at my house about three o'clock at
night . . . I felt well enough to take care of the service on
that same day, but was later on stricken with illness." We
should not deny any of the four virtues to this great missionary; but perhaps we should underline the courage, both
moral and physical, as a conspicuous characteristic of Henry
Melchior Muhlenberg.

VI

BENJAMIN RUSH

A Classical Doctor's Dilemma

*T*HOSE WHO HAVE READ to any extent in American Colonial history are impressed by the ideas and the activities of Benjamin Rush—a distinguished citizen who played a heroic part in the yellow fever epidemics of 1793 and 1797, in plague-ridden Philadelphia. The portrait of Rush by Charles Willson Peale reveals the essence of the man: independent, keen, with a blend of aristocratic reserve and democratic humanity. His theories and remedies are still debated in medical circles, but there is no doubt about his skill, his selflessness, and his devotion to all classes of sufferers. He is also well known as a signer of the Declaration of Independence and as an adviser to Thomas Paine in the writing of *Common Sense*. The medical school of the University of Pennsylvania and the Pennsylvania Hospital owed much to his efficient management. He developed new and more merciful methods of treating the insane. He contributed to the American Philosophical Society, and was elected a Fellow of the American Academy of Arts and Sciences.

Fortified by a basic belief in Divine guidance, Rush subscribed to a doctrine of "modified materialism," applied realistically the contemporary common sense philosophy, and rejected the theory of Innate Ideas. One of his main concerns was the scientific treatment of moral problems brought about by a junction of psychology with physiology. He was not a profound philosopher like Samuel Johnson of Connecticut. As one at home in the classics and history, however, he is a major contributor to the Colonial mind.

The style and phraseology of his *Autobiography* constitute one of the attractive offerings in our American records, and prove Rush to be an interesting blend of the pragmatist and the idealist. Amid countless down-to-earth situations, he described a dream in which he was visited by three historic characters. One of them said: "I am Solon"; the second: "I am William Penn"; the third: "I am Numa Pompilius." Another vision was a picture of Homer and Vergil coming back to earth in order to burn their own works because they were inferior to the Henriade of Voltaire! [1] Rush uses vivid expressions which hold the reader; when acting as chairman of a town meeting, he declared: "There was nothing in my heart that *vibrated* with the object of the meeting." [2] On another occasion he wrote: "Monarchies are illuminated by a *sun;* but republics should be illuminated only by *constellations* of great men."

Rush always liked an argument, and seems to have enjoyed opposition, especially with rival physicians. Rome, he humorously remarked,[3] was lucky because for several centuries its only practitioners of physic were either women or slaves. With grim sarcasm, he reported his supposed unpopularity in certain quarters: there was the *odium politicum,* the *odium theologicum,* and the *odium philologicum.* "The philologists hate me for writing against the dead languages." Another offence "was writing against monkish learning . . . by which I produced a confederacy of pedagogues against me." [4] Quarrels with Hamilton, Cobbett, Shippen, and even Washington (whom he placed below Gates in his estimate of military skill) left their scars on one who was externally proud and internally sensitive but always forthright and honest. Among those to whom he gave full confidence and affection were Franklin, Rittenhouse, John Adams, Jefferson, John Dickinson, and Anthony Benezet. And even in this group, we find Rush contradicting his devoted friends Adams and Jefferson on the subject of a required classical curriculum for grammar schools and colleges. Like Cato in his denunciation of Carthage, the Doctor wrote "Delenda est lingua Romana," in the educational system of Colonial America. We shall elaborate on this subject later and will find that it involves a curious paradox.

Rush, who was not a party man, took an occasional share in the stormy debates of the period. He opposed the weakness of a single chamber in the Pennsylvania constitution of 1776, and the absurdity of the so-called Council of Censors. To him, all was not serene in states where democracy might run riot, as it did in several lamentable cases. Socrates and Barnevelt, Rush pointed out, were put to death by assemblies that held their powers by the election of the people.[5] Sparta, with its "compound legislature," lasted five hundred years in an atmosphere of liberty. Athens and Rome "were disturbed by popular dissensions until a proper balance was found of senate and people." To Rush, the governor's veto was enough. Writing to Anthony Wayne, he complained about the Pennsylvania state constitution and the danger of either mob or Thirty Tyrants violence, but ended with a cheerful call to arms, from the *Odes* of Horace, which Wayne had read at the Academy: "De republica nunquam desperandum." [6] Even pagans could plan sensibly, Rush remarked. The history of the Greek commonwealths (which he praised more highly than many of the Founding Fathers did at the Convention of 1787) shows that human nature "has attained these degrees of perfection," [7] without Christianity. He was equally emphatic on the evils of relying on a single individual, whether a benevolent statesman or a tyrant. Rome suffered, as Cicero lamented, because of

Pompey's domination.[8] As rulers get more power, they tighten the reins: "Of so much consequence did the wise Athenians view the force of ancient habits in their laws that they punished with death all strangers who interfered in their policies." [9]

Rush published a tract on the evils of slavery, cooperating with the Quaker movement. He spoke out and wrote against the use of spirituous liquors and tobacco. This last concern was described with wry humor: "Smoking is merely a relief from the anguish which attends the inactivity and vacuum of the mind." He was a strong advocate for peace, remarking that if we had a War Office in time of peace, we should have a Peace Office in time of war. He voted against the death penalty, except in cases of willful murder. "From whence," he asked, "arose the conspiracies, with assassinations and poisonings which prevailed in the decline of the Roman Empire? Were they not favored by the public executions of the amphitheatre?" He advocated the study of the Bible in schools, and agreed with his friend John Adams in refusing to go to war with France over the "XYZ" scandal.

Rush was a deeply religious man, with an ancestral background of Quakerism, a Princeton Presbyterian training, a nonliturgical sympathy with the Episcopalian creed, and more than a casual interest in Universalism. He tells us that, while walking with some friends in his well-kept garden, he quoted to them the words of the grateful shepherd in Vergil's first Eclogue: *"Deus nobis haec otia fecit"*—it is God who has given us this happy estate.[10] He saw some merit in Paine's *Rights of Man,* but he regarded the *Age of Reason* as sheer atheism. To Benjamin Rush the French Revolution was a holocaust of spiritual and human relations. A sample prayer of his own making reads: "Incipienti, progredienti, proficienti sit mihi propitius Deus Bonus et Maximus" (May the good and great God bless me as I begin my tasks, make progress in them, and attain mastery!).[11] His family life was ideal in its affectionate relationships. He and his wife were a devoted couple, and two of his sons attained distinction in the service of the national government. Critical as he was of many persons and organizations, his home was a center of happiness and peace.

We have, however, a puzzle to solve: the reconciliation of his scepticism towards the standard classical curriculum, in contrast with his use of the Greco-Roman material for purposes of illustration. Like Telephus in the play of Sophocles, whose sore could be cured only by the spearpoint that wounded him, Rush records modern parallels for an infinite number of cases and problems from antiquity. In these instances he held the fort against Adams, who rode with him in the escort of honor which welcomed the New England members of the first Continental Congress, and against Jefferson, with whom he became politically reconciled, thanks to Rush himself, in the year 1811. Let us assemble Rush's own statements of his theory, and then present the cases where he seems to regard the ancient tradition as a workable example and a useful source of practical help, especially in the making of a literary style which compares favorably with any of our Colonial writers. And we may let him speak for himself.

Rush's own education was no less classical than that of his two friends mentioned above. Born at Byberry, near Philadelphia, in 1745, he was schooled at Samuel Finley's academy,[12] and was so well trained that he received advanced standing at Princeton: "In the spring of 1759 and in the 15th year of my age I was admitted to the Junior class." Samuel Davies, who became President in 1759, was commended by his pupil for having "introduced several new subjects of instruction into the college and given to the old branches of education a new and popular connexion." Rush defined him as Thomas Paine defined himself, "a self-made man—*faber suae fortunae.*" Rush attended Finley later as an apprentice physician in the latter's final illness, July 1776, and wrote to a classmate an account of Finley's last moments, quoting Vergil's *animus meminisse horret luctuque refugit*—"My mind is horror-struck at recollecting the scene, and shrinks from the sad thought of it." [13]

Rush and his classmate Ebenezer Hazard seemed to find their college Latin of some value. The latter suggested that after graduation they should correspond in Latin, but they gave up the idea because of its demand on their time. They had to content themselves with Latin tags and quotations, such as the handclasps of affection of which Vergil speaks.[14] But in 1765 Rush wrote that he was taking great pleasure in classical authors and had "of late read more physic [in Latin] than ever," and, in addition, was studying Hippocrates in the original Greek, "in which I find myself lamentably deficient." They prided themselves on their accuracy. A letter to Hazard in this same year[15] criticizes the thesis of a Doctor James Smith (later a professor at King's College) who marred the beauty of his discourse by his bad Latin: "His very paper of *errata* wants an *erratum*. Did you notice his *primo pagina?*"

In May 1765, when still a medical apprentice, he writes to his friend: "I am about to review some of my school authors, especially the Greek Testament and Horace, two books that in my opinion contain the marrow of the Greek and Latin languages." [16]

Rush, on graduation from Princeton, decided for a career in medicine, and became an apprentice to the distinguished Doctor Redman, whose death in 1808 he memorialized in Poulson's *American Daily Advertizer,* with a tribute from Ovid's *Amores,* freely rendered: "Sic nobis contingat vivere, sicque mori." [17] (May it be my lot thus to live and thus to die—as nobly as the master.) He received his medical degree at Edinburgh in 1768, with a Latin thesis *De Coctione Ciborum in Ventriculo (Dissertatio Physica Inauguralis,* dedicated to

Benjamin Franklin), "On the Digestion of Food in the Stomach;" in it he maintained that digestion was aided by natural stomach acids. He defended before the Edinburgh Medical Society a paper on bilious fever and venereal diseases, "in each of which I have ventured upon *loca nullo antea trita solo*—so far untrodden ground." [18] During his foreign study, residences, and travels in Europe he taught himself French, Italian, and Spanish, how thoroughly we do not know. In Edinburgh he might have employed Dr. John Brown, who "translated English themes into Latin for those graduates who were unable [or unwilling!] to do it themselves." [19] It looks, however, as if the learned translator was not called upon in Rush's case, because he states clearly in a letter to Dr. John Morgan "I am now busy translating my thesis." [20] It is quite probable that this Scottish rule of Latinizing theses may have prompted later statements by Rush that themes and inaugural addresses should be written and spoken in English.

The young doctor was welcomed and entertained by many prominent and cultivated persons. He staged a brilliant coup in persuading the Scotsman John Witherspoon to accept the Presidency of Princeton. Celebrating this event, he had recourse to Vergil's *redeunt Saturnia Regna*[21]—"Now the golden age has come again." He returned to take up the practice of medicine in Philadelphia, a young man of unusual promise.

There are several starting points in the scepticism of Benjamin Rush towards the Greco-Roman contributions to American culture. One is the curious resemblance of his theories to those of Hector St. John de Crèvecoeur. Rush agrees with the French immigrant on the freedom of America and its opportunities. "I had rather," said de Crèvecoeur, "admire the ample barn of one of our opulent farmers than study the dimensions of the Temple of Ceres." [22] Rush spoke similarly: "While the business of education in Europe consists of lectures upon the ruins of Palmyra and the antiquities of Herculaneum, or in disputes about Hebrew points, Greek particles, or the accent and quantity of the Roman language, the youth of America will be employed in acquiring those branches of knowledge which increase the conveniences of life, lessen human misery, improve our country, promote population, exalt the human understanding, and establish domestic, social, and political happiness."

For purposes of inculcating the religious element into the learning process, he calls for intensive study of the Bible: "If the years spent in teaching boys the Greek and Roman mythology were spent in teaching them Jewish antiquities and the connection between the types and prophecies of the Old Testament with the events of the New, don't you think we should have less infidelity and less immorality and bad government in the world?" This is a useful suggestion, but it is not a wise change if it means the elimination of the chief element in the culture of the Western world. He goes still further, goading his friend Adams: "Indeed, I owe nothing to the Latin and Greek classics but the turgid and affected style of my youthful compositions and a neglect of English." He holds that Hume and Swift were the main influences on his writing. Still more forthrightly he comments on the style of his own prose, which he asserted resulted from "having nearly forgotten the Greek and suspended for many years the delight which with I once read the Roman poets and historians." He takes pleasure in teasing his friend: "I often look back with regret upon the four years I spent at an academy on the borders of Maryland and Pennsylvania in learning the Greek and Latin languages; and had not my master taught me the duties of Christianity and given me the habits of *labor,* I should wish the memory of those years blotted out of my mind forever." Stating that he disapproved of the "manner in which Latin is taught," he made a still more explosive comment: "We do not stand in need now of Greek and Roman poets, historians, and orators.

Shakespeare, Thompson [sic], Pope, Hume, Robertson, Burke, Curran, Fénelon, Bourdaloue, and a dozen others could more than fill their places." This is a naïve disposal of Homer and Thucydides, Vergil and Tacitus. Is this friendly banter or missionary zeal? It did not change anyone's opinion or practice. Rush was impressed and wrote to Jefferson that Adams had been reading ancient philosophers and historians "in their *original languages,* for which he is a most strenuous advocate." [23] The doctor was attracted by the South Carolinian Arthur Middleton, who was educated in England and was "a critical Latin and Greek scholar," and "read Horace and other classicks during his recess from Congress." [24] Rush bows with mock stateliness to the versatile Philadelphian Francis Hopkinson, who was "not surpassed by Lucian, Swift, or Rabelais." [25]

On the positive side, Rush suggests a state university, and four colleges (in Philadelphia, Lancaster, Carlisle, and Pittsburgh). The first eight-year elementary period, according to Rush, should be devoted to speaking, reading and writing the English language, orally and without a grammar. Homer, Xenophon, Demosthenes, and Longinus were all taught to speak, read, and write their native tongue without the encumbrance of a textbook—"hence the sublimity, purity, and immortality of many of their writings." [26] After age twelve, the pupils should study natural history and geography, with French and German, orally only. Between the twelfth and fourteenth years, they should be grounded in elementary mathematics. From age fourteen to eighteen, they would have to deal with grammar, oratory, higher mathematics, philosophy, chemistry, metaphysics [!], chronology, history, government, agriculture, and manufactures. Rush makes one concession: the classical languages should be studied as special subjects during the last two years previous to the university as preparation for law, medicine, teaching, and a few other careers. Rush, and Paine also, argued that the Greek was a perfect language but was not learned through the medium of any other tongue. On its own merits, Rush held [27] that "Greek was used not less by an apple-woman than by the celebrated orators of Greece." The radical Paine had been guilty of a similar purple patch: "The best Greek linguist that now exists does not understand Greek as well as a Grecian plowman, or Latin as it was spoken by a milkmaid of the Romans." Rush further argued that "The writings of Voltaire were quoted by the hairdressers and milliners of Paris because they were written in the simple language of the country." We might question the linguistic accuracy of the Doctor, however, in his assertion: "The acquisition of words lessens the ability of the mind to acquire ideas." He would have profited by the methods recommended in Quintilian's *Institutio Oratoria*.

Most of Rush's criticisms of classical study are negative. We find, however, a constructive suggestion on a topic which is of primary importance today: [28] Rush believed in teaching a pupil to *read* Latin rather than to muddle over formal grammar. Pupils should not read ancient authors until the age of fourteen or fifteen, and only when they are necessary for professional careers, college purposes, and teaching. In such cases Rush optimistically predicts that he could read these masterpieces in the original with reasonable comfort. Even the casual reader, however, would raise the question whether the poet Persius (quoted often by the Dulanys of Maryland) could be understood without a good deal of scholarly assistance, not to mention a reliable dictionary.

We have been discussing Benjamin Rush's theories of education, amateurishly but emphatically stated and typical of his pragmatic temperament. Let us now turn to examine his *use* of this classical tradition. We shall find plenty of offhand echoes, natural in an honors student from a college which furnished so many clergymen, or lawyers, or holders of public office.

When the versatile doctor was concerned with the importance
of mastering skill in the speaking of English, and the writing
of the same, he had recourse to the *Ars Poetica* of Horace,
and disagreed with the ancient poet: [29] "The perfection of
the ear as an avenue of knowledge is not sufficiently known.
Ideas acquired through that organ are much more durable than
those acquired by the eyes: hence old men recollect voices
long after they forget faces." Whether this is correct pedagogy
or not is an open question. In any case, Horace thought otherwise:

> Segnius irritant animos demissa per aurem
> Quam quae sunt oculis subjecta fidelibus et quae
> Ipse sibi tradit spectator.

(Communications by the ear stimulate the mind less effec-
tively than those which are clearly set before the eyes, and
personally noted by the observer.) Here are two opposite
theories from the long history of education.

Horace appears often in Rush's letters and articles, as does
Cicero. Rush refers several times to the *De Officiis* of the
Roman orator.[30] A youth must be taught that "his life is not
his own when the safety of his country requires it." This
was a working motto; and the writer proves that "in the
commonwealths of Greece and Rome human nature, without
Christianity, attained a degree approaching perfection." In the
Doctor's *Influence of Physical Causes upon the Moral Faculty,*
we find a loan from Cicero,[31] recommending obedience to the
Law of Nature: "Est igitur haec, iudices, non scripta sed nata
lex, quam non didicimus, accepimus, legimus, verum ex natura
ipsa arripuimus, hausimus, expressimus, ad quam non docti
sed facti, non instituti sed imbuti sumus." (This, my lords, is
not a written but an innate law. We have not been taught it
by the learned; we have not received it from our ancestors;
we have not taken it from books; it is derived from nature

and stamped in invisible characters upon our very frame. It was not conveyed to us by instruction but wrought into our Constitution: it is the dictate of instinct.) This simply means (and it is the essence of all philosophy) obedience to the Higher Law as a guide for the human conscience to follow. Rush may have been dominating, and sometimes prejudiced, in his views; but we find him scholarly and accurate in his use of the sources, and possessed of an uncommonly good memory for the appropriate passages, especially from Horace, Cicero, Vergil, Lucretius, Terence, and Petronius. He cannot resist a tribute to Horace, "The Venusian poet who was blest by Genius and Philosophy."

This same receptivity is manifest in a brief memorandum on the meaning of "Common Sense" (*Sensus Communis*), which he asserted was not a faculty of the mind, but a matter of *feeling*. After examining the theories of Berkeley, Shaftesbury, Fénelon, Locke, Priestley, Reid, and others, he defines common sense as "opinions and feelings in unison with the opinions and feelings of the bulk of mankind." Here he is practically translating a passage from Cicero's *De Oratore*:[32] "In dicendo vitium vel maximum sit a volgari genere oratoris atque a consuetudine communis sensus abhorrere" (freely condensed by the editor as "The customary instinctive sense of what is required from all members of the same community"). Rush, who was always seeking a moral criterion, amended it further: "To think and act with the majority of mankind when they are *right,* and differing from them when they are wrong." This, he declares, "is the perfection of human wisdom and control." Physical and moral evils are "hydras" that require a Hercules to overcome them. Self-denial and austerity are needed always: even the "black broth" of the Spartans had its advantages for plain living.[33]

Tacitus appealed to Rush for many reasons. His critical viewpoint towards his contemporaries and his admiration of the historian's style prompted some special attention. Rush made careful notes of certain passages from the *Annals*. "The caprice of Fortune turns all human wisdom to a jest"; he dislikes "a ruler who is solitary more than one who passes his day in the glare of spectacles"; "Vespasian's reign brought simpler ways of living: the rich became frugal so as not to be plundered by the Emperor." "At the funeral procession of Cassius's widow the images of Brutus and Cassius were not displayed; but for that reason they were present to every imagination." In a letter to Samuel Miller, who wrote the definitive biography of Dr. John Rodgers, the beloved leader of Presbyterians in New York, Rush congratulates the author[34] on having happily imitated the manner of Tacitus in his memoir of Agricola, the incorruptible Roman governor. Rush likes, however, to point out the frailties of great men: [35] "I am sometimes disposed to question the talents of Caesar, the virtues of Antoninus, and the crimes of Commodus: I suspect Livy's well-concerted plans of battles were picked up in the barber shops of Rome or from deserters from the Roman armies."

The doctor went further than mere quotation. He published a brochure comparing the integrity of the Pennsylvania farmers with that of the Teutonic tribes as described in the *Germania*. He admired their chastity, their *sera iuvenum venus* (their sexual restraint), and their consequent hardiness, *robora parentum referunt,* reproducing the energy of their parents. All this was a contrast to Latin luxury and a lesson to the Romans.[36] Caesar, who knew these tribes well, expressed a similar opinion.[37]

Emotionally, Rush seems to have been deeply affected by Vergil. In a lecture *On Natural and Medical Sciences,* he harks back to the "Mantuan." [38] "I feel as Aeneas did when he was about to enter the gates of Avernus, but without a Sybil to instruct me in the mysteries that are before me." On a visit to France, seeing the paintings of Aeneas in various situations, he was impressed by the "moving history of his leaving Dido at Carthage," just as Aeneas himself was overcome with grief when he saw on the walls of the Phoenician palace the tragedy of Troy, and as Menelaus wept "when ten years after his return home he spoke of the deaths of the heroes."

Rush carefully recorded that Xenophon makes Cyrus declare,[39] in his last moments, that "the soul of man at the hour of death appears most divine and foresees something of future events." On the importance of light, he noted that "the flame of Prometheus's torch was the expression of a philosophic truth that did not escape the ancients." [40]

It is intriguing to note the large number of classical allusions in the writings of this cultivated scientist whose own education was based on "the learned languages." His mastery of English did not occur haphazard. Even as a young medical student he declared: *Studium sine calamo somnium*—"Study without pen in hand is an idle dream." His master Samuel Davies trained him to keep a commonplace book, "inserting such passages of the classics as struck me most forcibly on reading them." [41] This he called his Liber Selectorum.

As we dig deeper, we find more evidence of his essential classical knowledge, and his literary acumen. He once wrote that Lord Shaftesbury believed that "truth is so congenial to our minds that we love even the shadow of it"; and Horace[42] in his rules for composing an epic poem applied the same criticism, that "the fictions in poetry should resemble the truth." This is an exact reproduction of the "ficta voluptatis causa sint proxima veris" of the *Ars Poetica*. In 1768 Rush spoke of "well-doing and truth," as expressed in the Greek by Longinus in *On the Sublime*.[43]

His medical experience carried over into the problems of sanitation in preserving the health of the American troops. In contrast with what he denounced as the bungling neglect of the ill-equipped hospitals and the unsatisfactory conditions in the army, where he served for some time as head surgeon, Roman soldiers, he held, were healthy because they wore flannel shirts next to their skins and drank a mixture of water and vinegar[44] as contrasted with the unwholesome "grog" of modern times. Xenophon's care for his Ten Thousand, and the great Fabius the Delayer with his skillful retreats should serve as an example to later ages. In the fifth book of the *Aeneid,* Entellus the pugilist "lays away his arms, his boxing-gloves, and his shield;"[45] Rush quotes this passage to John Adams using it as a promise to say no more about his own "living in the enemy's country" and being the object of so much slander.

These jottings are indications of a ready-stocked mind. In his memorial address in praise of Rittenhouse, the speaker found a parallel describing the happy home life of the great scientist:[46] "Thus Sir Thomas Moore [sic] lived with his accomplished wife and daughter; thus Cicero educated his beloved daughter Tullia." Plutarch is called upon for an illustration of patriotism:[47] When Antipater demanded fifty of the Spartan children as hostages, "those wise republicans refused to comply . . . they offered him double the number of their adult citizens whose habits and prejudices could not be shaken by residing in a foreign country." Ancient proverbs flash out in Rush's correspondence. He had been waiting, like Horace's clown, till the stream of business should so far lessen that he could pass over it; Bacon's phrase *ipsa sapientia potestas est* struck him as profound. He was impressed by the proverb. "All the World's a Stage," and *Totus mundus histrionem agit.* He writes to the historian Ramsay: "Let us have some Athenian ostracism." There is a blend of Roman and Shakespearian in the adage: "We often ascribe good temper and benevolence to corpulency, and irascibility to sanguineous habits. Caesar thought himself safe in the friendship of the sleek-headed Anthony and Dolabella, but was afraid to trust to the professions of the slender Cassius." When discouraged with certain conditions in America, Rush agrees with "the Grecian general who proclaimed *Ossa mea non habebis* —he would prefer to be buried elsewhere than in his own country." [48] This thought had been expressed before in the case of the exiled Governor Hutchinson of Massachusetts Bay, and it was a fact in the case of Themistocles.

And yet, with all this interchange of classical allusions, Rush could not forget his old concern: when the "School of the Prophets," a group which later developed into the Presbyterian Seminary at Princeton,[49] began its meetings, he advised that "no more Latin should be learned in these schools than is necessary to translate that language into English, and no more Greek than is necessary to read the Greek Testament." This contrasts with the policy of the Lutheran Muhlenberg, who insisted on strict Latin tests for ministerial candidates. The metempsychosis of Pythagoras was cited [50] by the doctor as an illustration of changes in the human body. The profession to which Rush was dedicated was always near his heart; and he philosophized on the healing art in a letter to John Adams. Medicine, he maintained, was unlike music or poetry: it is a "mute art." There is a "mystery" here: when the old healer Iapyx cures the wound of Aeneas, with help from Olympus:

> Scire potestates herbarum usumque medendi
> Maluit et mutas agitare inglorious artes.

(He chose rather to know the potency of herbs and the practice of healing, and to deal in a silent art, unrenowned.) [51]

Rush himself was a modern healer, of minds and souls as well as of bodies. In his capacity as what we should today define as a psychiatrist, he considers the Emperor Domitian's habit of killing flies as a step to his numerous crimes of murder.[52] Anecdotes from Suetonius and Plutarch are too numerous in Rush's jottings to catalogue. On the pains and trials of Revolutionary days he had recourse to Addison's *Cato*. Writing to his patient wife, he said: "I should have blushed if Cato's house had stood secure and flourished in a civil war." [53]

Here, then, is the paradox. On the one hand we note Rush's recurring objection to the classics as a requirement in the school and college curriculum; on the other hand, we must recognize the zest with which the writer uses these ancient languages as vital and clarifying aids to style and to contemporary issues, whether political, religious, or literary. The probable answer is that Rush desired a humanistic method of teaching the classics rather than a mere presentation of grammatical forms and inflections. The Greco-Roman tradition had much to offer in the education of Americans, as a cultural element and an instrument of comparative progress. Rush was not contradicting himself when he remarked "I have no objection to the reading of the dead languages," which he himself cultivated with the greatest success. Rush always sought to clarify rather than complicate his method of approach to the classics. He criticized the Scottish philosophers who "were bewildered by the pagan doctrines of Aristotle and Plato," and in certain cases were getting dangerously close to Deism.[54] It was the pedantic presentation of the ancient masterpieces which he disapproved. They should be treated as literature, emphasizing the ideas rather than symbolic forms. This is what Rush himself aimed at: the application of the classical sources to the current life and thought of the new republic which he had done so much to promote.

VII

THOMAS PAINE

Was He Really Anti-classical?

THERE ARE THREE ways in which we may view the life and works of Thomas Paine. The first is that of the patriot who never lost his love for his adopted country and, with his *Common Sense* and *Crisis,* helped to found a nation. Secondly, there is the image of the would-be reformer of a world out of joint, the gadfly who irritated Burke and Pitt with his enthusiasm for the French Revolution and embarrassed his fellow Americans with his international indiscretions. Often inconsistent and at times unreliable, he took the whole universe as his field of activity. He might have said grandiloquently with Walt Whitman:

> Do I contradict myself?
> Very well, then I contradict myself:
> I am large, I contain multitudes.

It is the "third Paine" with whom we are here concerned. Paine was a gifted journalist, a stylist who set a high standard for critics and commentators. His attitude towards the Greek and Latin classics has never been analyzed as a part of the cultural atmosphere of the eighteenth century, nor with the development of a prose that expressed new ways of thinking

81

about old problems. His use of the ancient sources for purposes of illustration is just as clearly portrayed as it is in the orations of James Otis or in the notes of Thomas Jefferson. The significant difference was that Paine had recourse to translations, while Otis and Jefferson were at home in the original languages.

One of his biographers has remarked on the "timing" of Paine's communications: "His rise coincided with the development of popular journalism and the outbreak of the American Revolution—the first great political and social movement based on the theory and practice on the current support and power of the Common Man."[1] When Samuel Adams declared that Paine's *Common Sense* "popularized the principles of the Declaration," and when John Adams praised its style as "manly and striking," Paine egotistically agreed, and not without considerable justification: "It was the cause of America that made me an author—The force with which it struck my mind and the dangerous condition the country appeared to be in, by courting an impossible and unnatural reconciliation with those who were determined to reduce her—made it impossible for me to be silent—and if in the course of more than seven years I have rendered her any service, I have likewise added something to the reputation of literature by freely and disinterestedly employing it in the great cause of mankind, and showing that there may be genius without prostitution."[2] Another boast is similarly more downright: "I am proud to say that with a perseverance undismayed by difficulties, a disinterestedness that compelled respect, I have not only contributed to raise a new system of government . . . I have arrived at an eminence in political literature which aristocracy, with all its aids, has not been able to reach or rival."[3]

Purple patches like these are absurdly flamboyant but pardonable. Such claims irritated Paine's readers, notably Isaac D'Israeli, the bibliophile and literary historian who defined our pamphleteer in his *Curiosities of Literature* as "a very vulgar but acute genius whom we may suppose destitute of all delicacy or refinement, who tells us that the Sublime and the Ridiculous are so nearly related that it is difficult to class them separately." Paine himself commented on the distinction from the point of view of a master of epigram: "Where knowledge is a duty, ignorance is a crime." [4]

Thomas Paine was born at Thetford in Norfolk County, England, in 1737, the son of a Quaker stay-maker of excellent character but slender resources. The boy's sensitivity and his inferiority complex showed themselves throughout his career and many of his associates faded away because of his compensatory defiance. He was withdrawn from school at the age of thirteen to serve an apprenticeship to his father. Between this experience and his thirty-seventh year when Franklin in 1774, with his acute diagnosis of human character, gave Paine a letter of introduction to his son-in-law Richard Bache in Philadelphia, he had been a rolling stone. Unsuccessful stretches as an exciseman and as a tobacconist, a brief service on a British man-of-war, some schoolteaching and, whenever possible, attendance at scientific lectures, marked a long period of trial and error.

During his time as excise officer at Lewes he belonged to a workingman's club which met at the White Hart Inn.[5] The members discussed political and literary topics, and at the close of each meeting awarded a prize to the best debater. This was known as "The Headstrong Book," an old Greek Homer which the winner held until the next session. Paine was described by his associates as "The General of the Headstrong War" and was a frequent champion. At his interview with Franklin who was winding up his American agencies in London, Paine is said to have caught the fancy of "Poor Richard" by quoting the Latin proverb "Quisque suae fortunae faber" (Every man is the artisan of his own fortunes). This same motto was used by Captain John Smith, with the same punning significance ("faber" means "smith") when he assumed the guidance of the first settlers in Virginia. This epigram pleased Franklin and was used later when Paine claimed that he himself "began as the carver of his own fortune." [6]

However limited the adopted American was in his formal education, he did not disappoint his sponsor. After a few temporary jobs he became an editor and a journalist. He published in the *Pennsylvania Magazine,* and in other periodicals, general statements on democracy, the slave trade, women's rights, and copyright reforms; he also wrote popular science articles, presaging the great invention of his famous "pierless" iron bridge. He invoked ancient testimony against the practice of dueling. The Greeks and the Romans regarded the custom as a wrong one; they held, declared Paine, that an affair of private honor should not allow the personal element to interfere with the military spirit.[7] He slipped little phrases of classical origin into the text, as Poor Richard himself used to do: "The most virtuous woman is she who is least talked of" [8]—an adage which goes back to the funeral oration of Pericles and the Greek new comedy. He also interjected clichés such as the comparison of Washington with Fabius. These early writings served as preliminary practice for his attack on the larger and more dramatic issues of the day. Discussing the disgrace of Clive, who was crushed by his own tyrannical acts, he portrays him as, "some Heraclitus weeping for the world." [9]

Paine occasionally employed the dialogue form, as in an imaginary conversation between the ghosts of General Wolfe and General Gage, wherein the former chides the latter for his oppressive activities: "If you have any regard for the glory of the British name, and if you do not prefer the society of Grecian, Roman, or British heroes in the world of spirits to

the company of Jeffries, Kirk, and other royal executioners,
I conjure you immediately to resign your commission. Only
in a commonwealth can you find every man a patriot or a
hero. Aristides, Epaminondas, Pericles, Scipio, Camillus, would
have been nobodies if they had lived under royal govern-
ments." [10]

The essentially journalistic Paine applied his classical sources
sparingly and mostly from memory. Beginning in 1775 he had
the ear of Congress, signing his editorials in compliance with
the current fashion as *Aesop, Atlanticus, Vox Populi,* or *Hu-
manus.* These contributions were accompanied by *New Anecdotes of Alexander the Great, Cupid and Hymen,* and a re-
vised version of an earlier poem on the death of Wolfe; this
work portrayed Britannia mourning her universally beloved
leader, consoled by Mercury who reported that Wolfe had been
called into the ranks of the gods. All this was light stuff but
valuable apprenticeship. The writer should be credited with a
new and incisive type of persuasion.

Common Sense, which appeared on January 10, 1776, cleared
the way for general Colonial approval of separation from Great
Britain. It contained no reference to ancient history. Here was
a popular appeal aimed to enlighten soldiers round the campfires and civilians at their tasks of agriculture or industry. It
was a well-timed explosion and its contents offered little that
was novel to those who read Otis, Dickinson, Dulany, and
Jefferson's *Summary View.* Its feature was the vivid way in
which the grievances were stated. The demand for a republic
was stressed, defined later by the writer as Res Publica, "the
Public Good." [11]

The Crisis (which appeared December 23, 1776), offered
more of an analytical background after the famous opening
slogan, "These are the times that try men's souls." The second
number excoriated Lord Howe, "You hold out the sword of
war and call it the *Ultima ratio regum.*" [12] Britain has, like

Alexander, made war her sport and inflected misery for prodigality's sake." [13] The third *Crisis* reveals Paine's objection to a Quaker policy, which would "tie this continent to Britain like Hector to the chariot-wheels of Achilles." The fifth number, aimed at Sir William Howe, states matters even more strongly: "The histories of Alexander and Charles of Sweden are the histories of human devils." This tract is perhaps the most convincing one. It is a plea for freedom, comparing ancient and modern systems: "The wisdom, civil government, and sense of honor of the states of Greece and Rome are frequently held up as objects of excellence and imitation—But why do we need to go back two or three thousand years for lessons and examples? Clear away the mists of antiquity!" "The Greeks and Romans were strongly possessed of the spirit of liberty but not the principle . . . they enslaved the rest of mankind, though determined not to be slaves themselves."

The seventh installment gives us a hint of future transatlantic attempts by Paine to reform the British and French systems of statecraft: "My attachment is to all the world." It was the time, he felt, for nations to plan a program of peace and plenty: "The Alexanders and Caesars of antiquity have left behind them their monuments of destruction and are remembered with hatred . . . of more use was one philosopher, though a heathen, to the world than all the heathen conquerors that ever existed." In answer to comments by the Abbé Raynal he holds that "the idea of conquering countries, like the Greeks and Romans, does not now exist, and experience has exploded the notion of going to war for the sake of profit." [14] The thirteenth *Crisis* compares the inception of a peaceful United States in contrast to old Rome, which began "as a band of ruffians." [15] In any case, the Colonies should have been made independent in 1763, related to the mother country by loyalty alone—like the Greek settlements as described in the first book of Thucydides.

Paine felt that he had played a vital part in the development
of a few provinces into a world power. "If only Athens had
had the principle of *representation,* she would have surpassed
her own democracies." [16] The last *Crisis* appeared on December 9, 1783, and there were numerous celebrations of the
Peace. Paine turned poet with a ballad on "The Liberty-Tree"
and a song "Hail Great Republic." Despite certain complaints
about his persistent ego and his unkempt habits, we may be
grateful for his sincere belief in the promise of America and
courageous activities in her behalf during a critical decade.

He had not rested content with propaganda. He turned over
his royalties to the government. He enlisted in the "Flying
Camp." He served at Fort Lee as a brigade major. He was
elected secretary to the Committee on Foreign Affairs and to
the clerkship of the State Assembly. In spite of his various
ups and downs, one must admit that he deserved the honor
of election to the Philosophical Society, an honorary degree
from the University of Pennsylvania, and the gift of a farm
at New Rochelle, with a small honorarium from Congress.
He was never popular in the usual sense of the word. Franklin's daughter Sarah Bache wrote to her father in January
1781: "There was never a man less beloved in a place than
Paine in this, having at times disputed with everybody. The
most rational thing he could have done would have been to
die the instant he finished his *Common Sense,* for he never
again will have it in his power to leave the world with so
much credit." [17] He was seldom discreet, and it must be recorded that he had to resign his foreign affairs post because
he revealed little-known information concerning Silas Deane's
questionable arrangements with France. His position was more
justifiable, however, in regard to certain American problems. He argued that Virginia should give up her Western
territory for establishing new states. How could the Old Dominion claim a right to these lands "any more than the will

of Alexander could have taken it into his head to bequeath away the world?" [18] He stood for sound money and a chartered bank. On his return to England in 1787 he stepped into the limelight with an article, "Prospects on the Rubicon," expressing the hope that England would not embark on a costly war with France. "Democritus," he declared, "could scarcely have foregone laughing at that folly." [19] This was good advice; but Pitt, "a modern Julius Caesar," paid no attention to him. At this time the stay-maker's son from Thetford was on friendly terms with Burke and the Duke of Portland, and after demonstrating the quality of his iron bridge to prominent individuals and scientific groups, he was on the way to a successful career as an inventor. In America he had made suggestions for a "Continental Convention," and the proceedings of the 1787 Constitutional delegates were about to be ratified.

He had made also some remarks on fair taxation to meet state debts. He studied and wrote on the principles of "Agrarian Justice." But this peaceful situation turned to wrangling, primarily as a result of the taking of the Bastille and the radical messages from France, where "the world-child" had been adopted as a citizen and a representative from the department of Pas de Calais. The events making up this pathetic story are well known: first the publication of the *Rights of Man* and the *Age of Reason,* then the lawsuits and narrow escapes in England, and finally the enmity of Robespierre including a long period in the Luxembourg prison. Paine escaped the guillotine only because a citoyen, under orders, failed to chalk-mark the right door in the jail. His rescue by James Monroe, his hostility towards Gouverneur Morris, and his final restoration to favor by the French Assembly, are familiar topics. His bravery is beyond reproach, as in the case of his vote against the execution of the king. His distorted theology did not make clear the difference between Deism and Unitarianism, and his defiant agnosticism upset many believers.

It was not in order to call St. Paul a fool nor to describe the Madonna as a lineal descendant of the Ephesian Diana.[20]

In contrast with his successes in America, Paine met with disapproval in England. For example, Thomas Erskine, Paine's lawyer, quoted the passage from the satirist Lucian, where Jupiter and a countryman were chatting as they strolled together. Conversation proceeded comfortably until the latter contradicted the ruler of the gods, who then threatened him with a thunderbolt. "Jupiter," said the rustic, "you are always wrong when you invoke your thunder." [21] "In other words," remarked Erskine, "one can reason with the people of England, but cannot fight against the thunder of authority." Burke, with official England behind him, and even the Jacobin "Men of the Mountain," were all too much for the hopeful reformer.

When, however, we turn our attention again to the "Third Paine," to the self-appointed and self-educated journalist, and examine his writing, his background, and his philosophy, we find that the Thetford stay-maker's son deserves a hearing as a "classicist malgré lui." We ask, with John Adams, where he got that "clear, simple, and nervous style." When Gouverneur Morris, his chronic enemy, said of him, "He was ignorant even of grammar and polite usage," Morris was mistaken. For, if Paine attained any real distinction, it was in the mastery of brilliant style and a native ability to state his case with clarity and force. While he was in the modern channel with Defoe and Junius, his style was a creation of his own. It defies comparison. Like Thucydides, he witnessed the events about which he wrote; but those who compare him with Tacitus for vigor, irony, and terseness, are in error. We think of Sallust as a closer parallel.[22]

How was Paine able to hold his own (as he did) in competition with British and American university men or *philosophes* like Condorcet? The answer is that he was a voracious reader and debater who knew what would rouse his peers and reach his public whether they agreed or not. Also, how do we explain his frequent use of classical epigrams, with the absence of documented sources, at a time when many Americans recorded word for word the parallels to be found in the Greek or Latin masterpieces which furnished material to the men of the constitutional convention? Why does Paine use so many clichés and haphazard allusions to "the Madman of Macedon," or show praise for American democracy, and approval of certain pagan men of genius? What was really responsible for his abandonment of the usual offerings in the Thetford Grammar School, with its excellent preparation for the British universities? If we examine his record up to the age of thirty-seven when he crossed to America, we shall find out why and how. We may let Paine himself tell his story.

Paine's resistance to Latin grammar manifested itself early in his life. As a schoolboy he said: I "had no inclination to learn languages; but also because of the Quaker objection against the books in which the language was taught. This, however, did not prevent me from being acquainted with the subjects of all the Latin books used in the school." [23] It does not require much ingenuity to gather that this precocious, inquisitive, and restless lad, sitting in the same room with the reciting older boys, absorbed by secondhand osmosis much of the contents, if not the forms and syntax, of the older pupils' lessons. He had one ear on the teacher and the other in the land of his dreams.

We may query his statement about the Quaker viewpoint. William Penn at some length cited the pre-Socratic philosophers in order to enforce the doctrine of the Inner Light which was a basic part of the Friends' belief. George Fox, the founder of the sect, gave his blessing in 1676 to a Latin textbook, entitled *Institutiones pietatis, in usum Christianae juventutis scholasticae Latine redditae*. Anthony Benezet, the Philadelphia schoolmaster, approved Aesop, Plutarch, and many other classical authors whom he regarded as "safe." Paine might also have recollected that the William Penn Charter School offered courses in Latin with the full approval of the Meeting. Charles Thomson's copy of Ovid's *Metamorphoses* is a cherished relic in the school museum today. The disposition and temperament of our hero also indicate that he was perhaps dodging a task which in its early stages requires close and attentive study.

Paine's positive interests were clear enough: "The natural bent of my mind was to science." In an appeal to reason and liberty he quotes the old Greek proverb,[24] "What Archimedes said of the mechanical powers may be applied to these two qualities; had we a place to stand upon, we might raise the world." He maintained that an hereditary governor is as inconsistent as an hereditary author: "I know not whether Homer or Euclid had sons; but I will venture an opinion that if they had, and had left their works unfinished, these sons could not have completed them." [25] The quality of Homer or Euclid speaks for itself: it could not have been accomplished by anyone but a first class creative artist. Euclid is "a book of self-evident demonstration," independent of the author's identity. "I am not contending for the morality of Homer . . . a book of false glory . . . Aesop's moral is just, but the fable is cruel."

"Learning," he declared, "does not consist in the knowledge of languages, but in the knowledge of things to which language gives names. The Greeks were a learned people; but learning, with them, did not consist in speaking Greek any more than in a Roman's speaking Latin or a Frenchman's speaking French—From what we know of the Greeks, it does not appear that they knew or studied any language but their own —The schools of the Greeks were schools of science and philosophy, and not of languages; and it is in the knowledge of the things that science and philosophy teach, that learning

consists. Almost all the scientific learning that now exists came
from the Greeks, or the people that spoke the Greek language—It therefore became necessary to people of the other
nations that some among them should learn the Greek language, in order that the learning of the Greeks might be
known in those languages by translating the Greek books on
science and philosophy into the mother tongue of each nation."
Hence the study of Greek or Latin as such "was only the
drudgery business of a linguist." Hence also the danger of
putting the problem into the hands of specialists who force
it on the schools and colleges. "All honor to the great masters
who are deservedly cultivated, such as Aristotle, Socrates,
Plato, etc." But government should not set up a "factory of
notables." The mere name of antiquity establishes nothing.
Herodotus and Tacitus are important, and are judged according
to their inspirational interest; but they are credited only as far
as they relate things credible.[26]

It is clear to the reader that when Paine urges the abolition
of the dead languages and makes learning consist in scientific
knowledge, he leaves many blank pages in his program, and
the humanities get but a short shrift. He ignores contemporary
political scientists such as Locke.[27] To him, they represent
the machinery rather than the principles of statecraft. Locke
appears only once in a footnote; Montesquieu, Turgot, and
others are casually and seldom mentioned. Paine's view of the
Renaissance was myopic and he did not approach the ancient
masterpieces as works of beauty. He cared little for belles-
lettres or the literary criteria of style. Horace's immortal ode,
Eheu Fugaces, would not have stirred him as it did Benjamin
Rush. We must therefore make allowances for the blind side
of our Thetford prophet. Scholarly research in our modern
sense was foreign to him: "Of the numerous priests or parsons
of the present day—bishops and all—every one of these can
make a sermon or translate a scrap of Latin, even though
the subject has been rehearsed a thousand times before." Of

what use, he declares, are such pedantic *minutiae* when we have the translation before us?

In characteristic fashion Paine brings his argument to a climax: "As there is nothing new to be learned from the dead languages, all the useful books being already translated, it is a waste of time to study the originals. It is only in the living languages that new knowledge is to be found. A youth will learn more of a living language in one year than a dead language in seven." [28]

Paine therefore can be regarded as approving the ancient tongues, as well as their subject matter, through the medium of translations. It is the quality of the idea that matters. Homer, Aristotle, Demosthenes, and Cicero, considered as works of art, would have the same merit were they anonymous. The criterion is one of genius; and in the case of Homer, "the poet will remain, though the story be fabulous." [29] This is all reasonable enough, but very few persons can, or could, read Greek. But no true lover of poetry would believe that a translation of the text of the scene where Helen views the hostile host from the walls of Troy, or where Achilles is addressed by his chariot-horses, is adequate when compared with the original Homer. Jefferson, Adams, Otis, William Byrd, or James Logan, besides many of the clergy, such as the Mathers, were at home in the Greek language and also possessed a thorough acquaintance with Latin.

Our journalist's foreign language phobia was not confined to the classics. A period of ten years, spent mostly in France, should have been enough for the mastery of the Gallic tongue, both written and oral. [30] His speeches in the Convention and the Assembly, however, had to be relayed by an interpreter, translated from his English. If Joel Barlow and Gouverneur Morris felt at home in the language, why could not Paine have done likewise? With his alert wits he could soon have acquired at least a speaking acquaintance.

Despite his scepticism about the ancient tradition and its

application to contemporary life and thought, Paine indulged in many references to Greek or Roman examples. He found the pagan contribution to human progress in all departments of culture impressive. He had high praise for Solon's dictum that the most popular government was most satisfactory "when the least injury done to the meanest individual was considered as an insult to the whole Constitution."[31] Diogenes Laertius was noted by Paine as an authority on Persian religion.[32] Diodorus Siculus was welcomed as a commentator on the ancient calendars when "the moon was the first almanac."[33] Paine reported that the Thebans of Egypt[34] "measured the days according to the sun but not the moon." Herodotus, "who lived above 2200 years ago and is the most ancient historian whose works have reached our time," speaks of the stars as dividing the year into twelve months. All this is secondhand amateurish comment; but the ancient calendars caught the fancy of our starry reformer.

It is significant that Paine did not fail to record with admiration the famous definition by Cicero of the Law of Nature, unearthing it from Conyers Middleton's biography of the Roman orator: "The True Law . . . whoever will not obey it must first throw off the nature of man,"[35] "These," says Paine, "are the divine and forcible sentiments of Cicero . . . this is the fundamental, essential, and vital part of all true religion." It is one of the basic principles that played a part in our Colonial history. In item twenty-four of the *Theophilanthropos* tract, published in Paris in September 1796, we find "extracts from the moral thoughts of Theognis," a collection of Greek proverbs and satire which John Adams and Jefferson used in their discussion of the term *aristoi*.[36] With regard to a future state of the soul, we note the approval of Plato, Socrates, and Xenophon for its immortality. In the opinion of Cyrus the Great the soul becomes free from the flesh, while Christians include also the resurrection of the body.[37]

Paine is hortatory, realistic, rather than abstract or meta-physical. But his wide reading and his expressed admiration for Plato cause us to wonder whether he was not affected by the Theory of Ideas, when he wrote the following in his *Age of Reason:* "It may be said that man can make or draw a triangle, and therefore a triangle is a human invention. But the triangle when drawn is no other than the image of the principle: it is a delineation to the eye, and from thence to the mind, of a principle that would be otherwise imperceptible. All the properties of a triangle exist independently of the figure, and existed before any triangle was drawn or thought of by man." [38] Man had no more to do in the formation of those properties or principles than he had to do in making the laws by which the heavenly bodies move. The same thing applied, he held, to the principle of the lever or the wheel. The answer was "study the structure of the universe: this is the true theology—God's Creation!"

This excursion into philosophy is very suggestive. It is un-doubtedly true that Paine read Plato in translation. It is barely possible that he was familiar with Seneca's ninetieth Epistle, which had furnished material for moralizing in handbooks and extracts, and in discussing the inventions of early man. It might have also stemmed from the idealism of Bishop Berke-ley. Paine was a voracious if sometimes a superficial reader.

Our reformer in the field of the classics has high praise for Athenian democracy: "What Athens was in miniature, America will be in magnitude if only it follows the principle of representation." [39] He did not realize that Polybius was skeptical about pure democracies, and had raised the question whether the Attica of Pericles might not have resembled "a poorly-trimmed boat." [40] He found, however, "more to admire and less to condemn in that great people than in anything which history records." [41] He was mentally and physically at the farthest remove from the Oxford or Cambridge common-room atmosphere; yet, despite his lack of scholarly prominence, suggested a large-scale international group to study past and present contributions to world welfare. "A society for enquiring into the ancient state of the world and the state of ancient history, so far as history is connected with systems of religion ancient and modern, may be a useful and instructive institution." [42] This tradition must be kept in reasonable balance: "for if we travel still further into antiquity, there are a thousand authorities successively contradicting each other." Hence a respect but not an adoration of the men of old is in order. They should admire us rather than we them. "I have no notion," as Paine said on several occasions, "of yielding the palm of the United States to any Grecians or Romans that ever were born." [43]

NOTES

I. The Reverend Hugh Jones: A Spiritual Pragmatist

BIBLIOGRAPHY

Jones, Hugh, *Present State of Virginia,* ed. Richard L. Morton (Chapel Hill: University of North Carolina Press, 1956).

Laurens, Henry, *Narrative of His Voyage Capture and Imprisonment,* Collections o the South Carolina Historical Society (1857), I, 18–83.

Townsend, Sarah B., *An American Soldier: The Life of John Laurens* (Raleigh, North Carolina: Edwards & Broughton, 1958).

Wallace, D. D., *The Life of Henry Laurens* (New York, 1915).

NOTES

1. See the *Maryland Historical Magazine,* 18:159 (1923). The word "venerable" was added to his regular title.

2. See *The Papers of Benjamin Franklin,* ed. L. W. Labaree (New Haven, 1959, III, 324. Jones was one of his customers and donated some books to the Library Company of Philadelphia.

3. There is one copy in the British Museum and a photostat in the William and Mary College Library.

4. I.6.67-68.

5. See R. M. Gummere, *The American Colonial Mind and the Classical Tradition* (Cambridge, Massachusetts, 1963), chap. 4. The will of George Mason provided for a combination of classical and vocational studies for his nephews, who were not candidates for college.

6. See S. E. Morison, *By Land and by Sea* (New York, 1953), pp. 169-172.

7. A copy of this book (1746 edition) was also in Washington's library at Mount Vernon, autographed on the title page.

8. See D. D. Wallace, *The Life of Henry Laurens* (New York, 1915), pp. 16, 18, 133, 182, 183, 190, 434, 464.

9. *Ibid.*, p. 182.

10. *The Literary History of the American Revolution* (New York, 1897), II, 242-245.

11. See *Materials for History*, first series, ed. Frank Moore (New York, 1861), p. 227.

12. See Sara B. Townsend, *An American Soldier: The Life of John Laurens* (Raleigh, North Carolina, 1958), p. 25. Also *Letters on the American Revolution*, ed. F. R. Kirkland (New York, 1952), II, 13.

13. W. C. Taylor, ed. (London, 1843), p. 109 f. *Iliad*, IV.310-316. Townsend, pp. 37, 92.

14. In his *Essay on Translating Homer*.

15. Townsend, p. 123.

16. *Ibid.*, pp. 120-121.

17. *Ibid.*, p. 220. Horace, *Odes*, III.2.13.

II. ROBERT CALEF: CRITIC OF WITCHCRAFT

BIBLIOGRAPHY

Burr, George L., *Narratives of the Witchcraft Cases, 1648-1706* (New York, 1963).

Calef, Robert, *More Wonders of the Invisible World* (London, 1700; reprinted Salem, Massachusetts, 1796, 1823, etc.).

Drake, S. G., *The Witchcraft Delusion in New England*, 3 vols. (Roxbury, Massachusetts, 1866).

Fowler, Samuel P., ed., *Salem Witchcraft*, comprising *More Wonders of the Invisible World*, by Robert Calef, and *The Wonders of the Invisible World*, by Cotton Mather (Salem, Massachusetts, 1861).

Kittredge, George L., *Witchcraft in Old and New England* (Cambridge, Massachusetts, 1929).

Mather, Cotton, *Memorable Providences Relating to Witchcrafts and Possessions* (Boston, 1689).

———— *The Wonders of the Invisible World* (Boston, 1693).

Mather, Increase, *Cases of Conscience Concerning Evil Spirits* (Boston, 1698).

———— *Essay for the Recording of Illustrious Providences* (Boston, 1684).

Poole, William F., *Cotton Mather and Salem Witchcraft* (Boston, 1869).

Sibley, John L., *Biographical Sketches of Graduates of Harvard University,* Vols. I and II (Cambridge, Massachusetts, 1873, etc.).

Starkey, Marion L., *The Devil in Massachusetts* (New York, 1949).

Upham, Charles W., *Salem Witchcraft,* 2 vols. (Boston, 1867).

NOTES

1. *Daemonologie,* a treatise published in 1599, denouncing witchcraft and backing up the civil authorities in suppressing it.

2. Horace, *Odes,* I.3.25-26.

3. T. Hutchinson, *The History of the . . . Massachusetts-Bay,* ed. L. S. Mayo (Cambridge, Massachusetts, 1936), II, 41n.

4. *Epistles,* I.2.69.

5. Juvenal, *Satires,* trans. G. G. Ramsay, Loeb Classical Library, XIII, 223-224.

6. Ovid, *Metamorphoses,* VII.202. For Claudia, see Ovid, *Fasti,* IV.305 ff. For Tuccia, see Pliny, *Natural History,* XXVIII.12.

7. *Aeneid,* VI.586. For Canidia, see Horace, *Satires,* I.8.24.

8. Thessaly was notorious for its sorceries and spells.

9. Tacitus, *Annals,* trans. Michael Grant (London: Cassell 1963), II.69 ff.; III.1-6.

10. Johannes Trithemius, Abbot of the Benedictine monastery of Würzburg, who wrote a book against sorcery in 1508: *Antipalus Maleficiorum.*

11. Evil princes of the Hebrew underworld. Apollyon is "The Destroyer" in *Pilgrim's Progress.*

12. For some of these miraculous cases, see Philostratus, *Life of Apollonius of Tyana,* trans. F. C. Conybeare, Loeb Classical Library, I, 257, 365, 407, 491; II, 91, 143, and *passim.* Justin Martyr, *Opera Omnia,* ed. Johann K. T. Otto (Jena, 1881), vol. III, pt. II, 34 ff.

13. The Elder Seneca and the rhetorician Quintilian were both teachers of oratory and natives of Spain.

14. That is, one completely in the power of the Evil One as contrasted with one not really touched by the curse.

III. Michael Wigglesworth:
From Kill-joy to Comforter

BIBLIOGRAPHY

Crowder, Richard, *No Featherbed to Heaven* (East Lansing: Michigan State University Press, 1962); title taken from Wigglesworth's *Meat out of the Eater.*

Dean, John Ward, *Memoir of the Reverend Michael Wigglesworth* (Boston, 1871; reprinted Harper Torchbooks, New York, 1965).

Morgan, E. S. ed., *The Diary of Michael Wigglesworth, 1653-1657*, Publications of the Colonial Society of Massachusetts, vol. 35 (1946), pp. 311-444.

Sibley, J. L., *Biographical Sketches of Graduates of Harvard* (Cambridge, Massachusetts, 1873), I, 259-286.

Wigglesworth, Michael, *The Day of Doom . . . with Other Poems*, ed. K. B. Murdock (New York: Spiral Press, 1929).

NOTES

1. A dialect form, as in "The penniless parliament of threedbare poets," by J. Beale, 1637.

2. For a sketch of Cheever, see S. E. Morison, *Builders of the Bay Colony* (Boston, 1930).

3. See Quintilian, *Institutio oratoria,* Bk. IV.

4. See Crowder, *No Featherbed to Heaven,* pp. 211-212.

5. For these candidacies and offers, see Sibley, *Biographical Sketches of Graduates of Harvard,* I, 269; and Morgan, *The Diary of Michael Wigglesworth,* pp. 328, 335, 359, 363.

6. *Video meliora proboque, deteriora sequor,* from *Metamorphoses,* trans. F. J. Miller, Loeb Classical Library, VII, 20-21.

7. For some of these self-reproaching passages, see Morgan, p. 323 and *passim.*

8. Morgan, p. 370.

9. *Ibid.,* p. 315.

10. Wigglesworth, *The Day of Doom,* pp. viii-xi.

11. Moses Coit Tyler, *History of American Literature* (New York, 1897), II, 34.

12. Wigglesworth, p. iii.

13. For John Cotton's similar attitude, see R. M. Gummere, *The American Colonial Mind and the Classical Tradition,* chap. 3.

14. *Pythian Ode,* VIII.135 ("Man is but the dream of a shadow").
15. See Crowder, pp. 180, 192, 194, and *passim.*
16. *Ibid.,* p. 152.

IV. SAMUEL DAVIES: A VOICE FOR RELIGIOUS FREEDOM

BIBLIOGRAPHY

Davies, Samuel, *Sermons,* 3 vols. (Philadelphia, 1864). For some selected but not complete classical references in the sermons of Davies, see I, 80-81, 206, 308, 314, 454, 499, 606, 618, 627; II, 39, 107, 147, 261, 274, 386, 574; III, 74, 84, 89, 172-191, 339, 388-395, 482, 490, 523 ff.
Foote, W. H., *Sketches of Virginia* (Philadelphia, 1850), 1, 157-307.
MacLean, John, *History of the College of New Jersey* (Philadelphia, 1877), I, 219-248.

NOTES

1. For these anecdotes, see W. H. Foote, *Sketches of Virginia,* I, 199, 232, 243-244, 255. Also Horace, *Odes,* I.3.8. *Epistles,* I.II.27, I.5.28. Vergil, *Aeneid,* III.56-57, and *passim.*
2. Suetonius, *Vespasian,* trans. J. C. Rolfe, Loeb Classical Library, IV. Tacitus, *Histories,* V.13. Davies, *Sermons,* I, 293.
3. Horace, *Odes,* III.5.7. Davies, *Sermons,* III, 156.
4. *Satires,* II.2.79. Vergil, *Aeneid,* VI.747. Davies, *Sermons,* II, 42.
5. Pindar, *Pythian Ode,* II.173-175. Euripides, *Bacchae,* p. 795. Terence, *Phormio,* I.2.28. Davies, *Sermons,* II, 540.
6. *Odes,* II.17.9-10.
7. Cicero, *De natura deorum,* I.3.
8. *Ibid.,* I.115.
9. For example, Seneca, *Naturales quaestiones,* VII.1. Hesiod, *Works and Days,* 238 ff. Cicero, *De Divinatione, passim.*
10. *Satires,* I.166-167. Davies, *Sermons,* I, 361.
11. *Aeneid,* VI.625-627.
12. *Ars poetica,* pp. 180-181.
13. Plutarch, *Lives,* trans. B. Perrin, Loeb Classical Library, VII.58. Davies, *Sermons,* I, 345.
14. Seneca, *Epistles,* 84.12, 94.73. Davies, *Sermons,* I, 268.
15. Davies, *Sermons,* III, 351.

V. HENRY MELCHOIR MUHLENBERG:
A SPIRITUAL TROUBLE-SHOOTER

BIBLIOGRAPHY

Mann, W. J., *Life and Times of Henry Melchior Muhlenberg* (Philadelphia, 1888).
Muhlenberg, Henry M., *Journals,* trans. T. G. Tappert and J. W. Doberstein, 3 vols. (Philadelphia: The Muhlenberg Press, 1942-1958).
Richards, H. M. M., *The Descendants of Henry Melchior Muhlenberg* (Lancaster, Pennsylvania: German-American Society, 1960).
Tappert, T. G. and J. W. Doberstein, *The Notebook of a Colonial Clergyman* (Philadelphia, The Muhlenberg Press, 1959), condensed from Henry Muhlenberg, *Journals.*
Wallace, Paul A. W., *The Muhlenbergs of Pennsylvania* (Philadelphia: University of Pennsylvania Press, 1950).

NOTES

1. So described by Paul A. W. Wallace, *The Muhlenbergs of Pennsylvania,* p. 50. I am much indebted to this excellent biography.
2. See Wallace, *Muhlenbergs,* p. 48.
3. See Quintilian, *Institutio oratoria,* trans. H. E. Butler, Loeb Classical Library, 1.9.1, III, *passim,* for such terms as *methodicé, historicé.* We note also *juridicial, demonstrative, deliberative, forensic,* etc. Aristotle divided oratory into *forensic, deliberative* and *demonstrative.*
4. See R. M. Gummere, "Apollo on Locust Street," *Pennsylvania Magazine of History and Biography,* 56:68-92 (1932).
5. Muhlenberg, *Journals,* I, 244.
6. For current tracts, articles and debates, see Charles R. Hildeburn, *A Century of Printing: The Issues of the Press in Pennsylvania, 1685-1784* (Philadelphia, 1885).
7. For the reputation of the teaching at Bethlehem, see *The Virginia Magazine of History and Biography,* 11:117 (1903).
8. Journal entry for November 23, 1762. Presumably Peletiah Webster, class of 1746 at Yale, who gave up his New England parish in 1755 for business and journalism, resided for some years in Philadelphia, and was a strong advocate of the Constitution. He is

known to have visited Charleston, South Carolina, in 1765. See
Publications of the Southern History Association, II, 131-148 (1898).
Also Anson Phelps Stokes's *Memorials of Eminent Yale Men* (New
Haven, Connecticut, 1914), pp. 150-157. Webster taught for a
short time at the Germantown Academy in Philadelphia.

9. This was Erdman Uhse, a "polyhistor" who became a Master
of Philosophy at Leipzig in 1698 and wrote (ninth edition, 1727)
the handbook mentioned above, containing questions and answers
on the style and the delivery of sermons and orations.

10. *Ars poetica,* p. 5.

11. For Taylor's application of this same figure, see R. M. Gummere, *The American Colonial Mind and the Classical Tradition,*
p. 155, n. 14.

12. See *Odyssey,* 24.68-70. J. G. Frazer, *The Golden Bough* (London, 1890), *passim;* F. B. Gummere, *The Beginnings of Poetry*
(New York, 1901), pp. 223-224.

13. Quoting Jerome's "Heresies must be cut off not by human
law but by the Sword of the Spirit." See Jerome, *In Jeremiam;*
S. Hieronymi, *Opera omnia,* vol. 24, no. 4 from Jacques P. Migne's
Patrologiae Cursus completus.

14. See *The Travels of William Bartram* (New York, 1928), p.
26.

15. Benjamin Rush, *Essays* (Philalelphia, 1806), pp. 238-239.

16. See H. M. M. Richards, *The Descendants of Henry Melchior
Muhlenberg.* Also W. J. Mann, *Life and Times of Henry Melchior
Muhlenberg,* p. 437 ff.

VI. BENJAMIN RUSH: A CLASSICAL DOCTOR'S DILEMMA

BIBLIOGRAPHY

Goodman, N. G., *Benjamin Rush, Physician and Citizen* (Philadelphia, 1934).

Rush, Benjamin, *The Autobiography of Benjamin Rush,* ed. G. W.
Corner (Princeton, New Jersey, 1948).

———— *Benjamin Rush, a Memorial . . . Written by Himself,* ed.
L. A. Biddle (Philadelphia, 1905).

———— *Essays, Literary, Moral, and Philosophical* (Philadelphia,
1806).

—— *Letters of Benjamin Rush,* ed. L. H. Butterfield, 2 vols. (Princeton: Princeton University Press, 1951).

—— The *Selected Writings of Benjamin Rush,* ed. D. D. Runes (New York: Philosophical Library, 1947).

For Rush as a medical practitioner, see:

Binger, Carl, *Revolutionary Doctor: A Portrait of Benjamin Rush 1746-1813* (New York, 1966).

Shryock, Richard H., *Medicine in America* (Baltimore, 1966).

For his interest in philosophy and metaphysics, see:

Riley, I. Woodbridge, *American Philosophy: The Early Schools* (New York, 1907).

—— *American Thought, from Puritanism to Pragmatism* (New York, 1915).

NOTES

1. *Letters,* II, 1167, 1170.
2. *Memorial,* p. 189. Also *Letters,* I, 220.
3. *Selected Writings,* p. 285.
4. *Letters,* II, 1061, 1114.
5. *Letters,* I, 220. *Selected Writings,* pp. 59, 68.
6. Horace, *Odes,* I.7.27. *Letters,* I, 148.
7. *Selected Writings,* p. 91.
8. *Letters,* I, 191, 544.
9. This law was mentioned at the Constitutional Convention by Charles Pinckney; see Jonathan Elliot, editor, *Debates on the Adoption of the Federal Constitution* (Philadelphia, 1845), V, 398. See also *Essays,* p. 148.
10. *Memorial,* p. 195.
11. Autobiography, pp. 277, 291.
12. Autobiography, pp. 28-37. *Essays,* pp. 21-56.
13. *Aeneid,* II.12. *Letters,* I, 24.
14. *Aeneid,* I.408-9. *Letters,* I, 6.
15. *Letters,* I, 21.
16. *Ibid.,* I, 14.
17. *Amores,* I.3.17-18. *Letters,* II, 946.
18. From Lucretius, *De rerum natura,* I.926-927.
19. *Autobiography,* pp. 44, 89.
20. *Letters,* I, 50.
21. *Eclogues,* IV.6.

22. *Letters from an American Farmer* (New York, 1912), p. 10 ff. Also, R. M. Gummere, "Apollo on Locust Street," *Pennsylvania Magazine of History and Biography*, 56:83-85 (January, 1932). And *Letters*, I, 494, 524-525; II, 1066 ff.

23. *Letters*, II, 1079.

24. *Autobiography*, p. 153.

25. *Ibid.*, p. 192.

26. *Essays*, pp. 15-16, 26, 46.

27. *Ibid.*, p. 26.

28. *Ibid.*, pp. 52-55. See a letter to Rush from the Reverend James Muir of Alexandria in 1791, who claimed satisfactory results from this comprehensive type of reading. Letters, I, 604-607.

29. *Essays*, p. 47. Horace, *Ars poetica*, pp. 180-182.

30. *Selected Writings*, p. 90. Cicero, *De officiis*, II.44. *Essays*, pp. 10-12.

31. *Selected Writings*, p. 181. Cicero, *Pro Milone*, p. 4.

32. III.12, ed. A. S. Wilkins. *Essays*, pp. 249-255.

33. *Essays*, p. 13.

34. *Letters*, II, 1193. Autobiography, p. 333 ff. *Annals*, trans. Arthur Murphy (London, 1793), III, 18.55.76. Also Tacitus, *Dialogus*, chap. 25. *Letters*, II, 989. *Essays*, pp. 226-248.

35. *Letters*, I, 534.

36. *Selected Writings*, pp. 258-260, 289.

37. *De bello Gallico*, VI.21.

38. *Selected Writings*, p. 192.

39. *Ibid.*, p. 187n.

40. *Ibid.*, p. 138n.

41. *Autobiography*, p. 36.

42. *Essays*, p. 96. *Ars poetica*, p. 338.

43. I.2. *Letters*, I, 56.

44. *Letters*, I, 142-143 (Caesar fed his troops on boiled wheat instead of flour).

45. *Ibid.*, II.1117. *Aeneid*, V.484.

46. *Essays*, p. 359.

47. *Ibid.*, p. 7. See Montaigne, *Complete Works*, trans. Cotton (London, 1700), p. 89.

48. See, for example, Seneca, *Epistles*, 86, where Scipio rebukes his own ungrateful country. Also *Letters*, II, 1182; II, 912, 936. *Selected Writings*, p. 183.

49. *Letters*, II, 946.

50. *Selected Writings,* p. 336.
51. *Letters,* II, 1108. Vergil, *Aeneid,* trans. Mackail, XII.396-397.
52. *Selected Writings,* p. 205.
53. *Letters,* I, 101-102, quoting from Act IV, Scene I. For loyalty to Juba, see Act IV, Scene 4. *Letters* I, 198.
54. *Letters,* II, 1075.

VII. THOMAS PAINE: WAS HE REALLY ANTI-CLASSICAL?

BIBLIOGRAPHY

Aldridge, Alfred O., *Man of Reason: The Life of Thomas Paine* (Philadelphia, 1959).

Best, Mary A., *Thomas Paine, Prophet and Martyr of Democracy* (New York, 1927).

Gould, F. J., *Thomas Paine* (London, 1925).

Paine, Thomas, *Political Writings,* 2 vols. (Charlestown, 1824).

Peach, Arthur W., *Selections from the Works of Thomas Paine* (New York, 1928).

van der Weyde, W. M., *The Life and Works of Thomas Paine,* (New York: Paine National Historical Association, 1925).

NOTES

1. Aldridge, *Man of Reason: The Life of Thomas Paine,* p. 27.
2. *The Crisis,* no. 15 (April 19, 1783), quoted in van der Weyde, *Life and Works of Thomas Paine,* III, 246-247.
3. van der Weyde, VII, 17.
4. *Ibid.,* IV, 272; VIII, 143.
5. Best, *Thomas Paine,* p. 16.
6. *The Rights of Man,* Pt. 2, chap. 5, in van der Weyde, I, 6; VII, 16.
7. *The Pennsylvania Magazine* (May 1775).
8. *Letter to the Female Sex,* in van der Weyde, II, 91. See Thucydides, trans. C. F. Smith, Loeb Classical Library, I, 341.
9. *The Pennsylvania Magazine* (May 1775).
10. See van der Weyde, II, 15-16, 259.
11. *Ibid.,* VI, 268.

12. For the same Latin phrase, see *The Rights of Man,* Pt. 2, chap. 5, in van der Weyde, VII, I.

13. *The Crisis,* no. 2, in van der Weyde, II, 294.

14. See van der Weyde, IV, 170, 198. See also Best, p. 202.

15. *Ibid.,* III, 239.

16. This is a sweeping statement, and an incorrect one. For a study of ancient representation, see J. A. O. Larsen, *Representative Government in Greek and Roman History* (Berkeley, California, 1955).

17. Quoted in Aldridge, p. 86.

18. See van der Weyde, IV, 93.

19. "The Laughing Philosopher," contrasted with Heraclitus "The Weeping Philosopher," see van der Weyde, IV, 322.

20. Peach, *Selections from the Works of Thomas Paine,* p. 234.

21. See van der Weyde, I, 296. Lucian, *Zeus Catechized,* trans. A. M. Harmon, Loeb Classical Library, II, 79.

22. Aldridge, p. 44 ff.

23. For passages dealing with Paine's anti-linguistic viewpoint, see van der Weyde, I, 4-6; VIII, 58-69, 252-253. Peach, pp. 259-264, 290-291.

24. Paine, *Political Writings* (Charlestown, 1824), II, 153. Also van der Weyde, VI, 231.

25. F. J. Gould, *Thomas Paine,* p. 93. Peach, pp. 315, 361.

26. See van der Weyde, V, 229. Peach, p. 291.

27. See Aldridge, p. 40. Paine did not use these authorities as background. He claimed credit for an original approach. For his opinion of some of these men, especially the French *philosophes,* see *Political Writings,* II, 96-97.

28. Benjamin Rush, a Princeton honors graduate, thought likewise on this subject. See his *Essays,* p. 55.

29. See van der Weyde, VIII, 116-117. Peach, p. 290-291.

30. Gould, p. 106, "Paine never attempted to speak more than a sentence or two in French."

31. Perhaps a reference to Plutarch's *Solon,* chap. 18.

32. See van der Weyde, IX, 42.

33. Bk. I, chap. 2, trans. C. H. Oldfather, Loeb Classical Library, IX, 67.

34. See van der Weyde, IX, 62 ff.

35. *Ibid.,* IX, 275-280.

36. *Ibid.,* VIII, 347.
37. *Ibid.,* IX, 72.
38. *Ibid.,* VIII, 53-56. Peach, p. 256 f.
39. See van der Weyde, VI, 272-273.
40. For the use of this figure, see R. M. Gummere, *The American Colonial Mind and the Classical Tradition,* pp. 177-178.
41. See van der Weyde, VI, 266.
42. *Ibid.,* IX, 125. Gould, pp. 170-171.
43. From *The Crisis,* no. 5.

Index

Adams, John, v, 8, 89, 93, 94; friendship with Rush, 66, 67, 68, 71, 72, 78, 79; praise for *Common Sense,* 82

Adams, Samuel, ix, 43; on *Common Sense,* 82

Addison, Joseph, 6; his *Cato,* 6, 80

Aeschylus, 28

Aesop, 91

American Academy of Arts and Sciences, 64

American Antiquarian Society, 15

American Daily Advertiser, 69

American Philosophical Society, 7, 53, 64, 87

American Revolution, 82

Ancient and Honorable Artillery, 40

Andros, Sir Edmund, 15–16

Anglican Church, *see* Church of England

Antipater, 78

Apollonius of Tyana, 23

Archimedes, 91

Aristides, 85

Aristotle, vii, 28, 33, 42, 80, 92, 93

Arminianism, vii, 30

Arnold, Matthew, 9

Augsburg Confession, 51

Aurelius, Marcus, 6, 20

Bache, Richard, 83

Bache, Sarah, 87

Bacon, Sir Francis, 28, 78

Barlow, Joel, 93

Bartram, William, viii, 61

Bellomont, Lord, 17

Benezet, Anthony, 66, 90–91

Berkeley, George, 75

Beveridge, John, 53

Beverley, Robert, his *History and Present State of Virginia,* 1

Blair, James, 1–2

Blair, Samuel, 41

Bodin, Jean, 23

Body of Liberties, Massachusetts, vi

Boston Gazette, 43

Boston Latin School, 27

Bourdaloue, Louis, 72

Braddock, Edward, 44

Bradstreet, Anne, 35

Brattle, Thomas, 13

Brown, Dr. John, 70

Burke, Edmund, 72, 81, 88, 89
Burroughs, Reverend George, 14–15
Byrd, William, ix, 1, 61, 93

Caesar, Julius, 62, 76, 88
Calef, Robert, 12–24; attitude toward witchcraft, 17; *More Wonders of the Invisible World,* 17, 23; and superstition, 22–23
Calef, Robert, Jr., 17
Callimachus, 62
Calvert, Leonard, 2
Calvinism, 25, 34
Camillus, 85
Carrier, Martha, 14
Catiline, 53
Cato, 66
Chapman, George, 9
Chauncy, Charles, 34
Cheever, Ezekiel, 27–28
Church of England, 42, 60
Cicero, vii, 19, 28, 45, 62, 66–67, 75, 78, 93; *De natura deorum,* 46–47; *De Divinatione,* 47; *De Officiis,* 74; *De Oratore,* 75
Clive, Robert, 84
Cobbett, William, 65
Colden, Cadwallader, viii
College of New Jersey, 41. *See also* Princeton University
Condorcet, Marie Jean Antoine Nicholas de Caritat, Marquis de, 89
Congregational Constitution, 53
Constantine, 44
Continental Congress, 7, 58, 68; suggested by Paine, 88
Corey, Giles, 14
Cornwallis, Charles, 7
Cowper, William, vi
Creek Indians, 62
Crèvecoeur, J. Hector St. John, 70
Curran, John Philpot, 72

Cyrus the Great, 94

Dante, 45
Davenport, John, 20, 26
Davies, Samuel, 41–49, 77; European travels, 42–43; *The Mediatorial Kingdom,* 44; patriotism, 44; *General Resurrection,* 45; and classicism, 45–49; *Rule of Equity,* 45; *Practical Atheism Exposed,* 46; *Miracles and Portents,* 47; *Signs of the Times,* 47; President of Princeton, 68
Day, Thomas, 11
Deane, Silas, 87
Declaration of Independence, 64
Defoe, Daniel, 89
Deism, vii, 5, 30, 80, 88
Democritus, 88
Demosthenes, 29, 44, 72, 93
Dickinson, John, 66, 85
Dinwiddie, Robert, 42
Diodorus Siculus, 94
Diogenes Laertius, 94
D'Israeli, Isaac, 82; his *Amenities of Literature,* viii; his *Curiosities of Literature,* 83
Dixon, Jeremiah, 3
Doddridge, Philip, 43
Domitian, Roman emperor, 79
Donne, John, 34
Drayton, John, 11
Drayton, William Henry, 11
Duché, Jacob, 58
Dulany, Daniel, 73, 85
Dunster, Henry, 27

Eaton, Theophilus, 26
Edinburgh Medical Society, 70
Edwards, Jonathan, 25, 28, 34, 39, 45
Emerson, Ralph Waldo, 26, 40; his *Essay on Intellect,* vii; *Lecture on the Times,* 26
Emmanuel College, 32
Epaminondas, 85

Epicurus, 19, 47
Erskine, Thomas, 89
Euclid, 91
Euripides, 46
Eutropius, 62

Fagg's Manor School, 41
Fairfax, Sally, 5–6
Fairfax, Thomas, 5–6
Fénelon, François de Salignac de La Mothe-, 72, 75
Finley, Samuel, 68
Fox, George, 90
Francke, Augustus, 52
Franklin, Benjamin, viii, 3, 8, 59; and Rush, 66, 70; and Paine, 83–84
Franklin College (Franklin and Marshall), 62
French and Indian wars, 44, 47
French Revolution, 67, 81

Gage, General Thomas, 84
Gates, Horatio, 65
Gentleman's Magazine, 2
George II, king of England, 52, 61
George III, king of England, 48
Germanicus, 21
Gersdorf, Baroness von, 51
Gibbon, Edward, 8
Gooch, Sir William, 42

Hale, Reverend John, his *Modest Enquiry,* 18
Hamilton, Alexander, 65
Harvard College, 17, 25, 27, 28, 31, 33, 39
Hawthorne, Nathaniel, his *Scarlet Letter,* 15
Haynes, John, 32
Hazard, Ebenezer, 69
Herodotus, 62, 92, 94
Hesiod, 28
Higginson, John, 14
Hippocrates, 69
Homer, 9, 23, 28, 47, 62, 72, 91, 93

Hooker, Reverend Samuel, 29
Hopkinson, Francis, 5, 51, 72
Horace, 18, 20–21, 23, 28, 43, 44, 46, 47, 62, 69; his *Epistles,* 3; his *Risum teneatis,* 56; his *Odes,* 66; his *Ars Poetica,* 74; *Eheu Fugaces,* 92
Howe, Sir William, 85
Hume, David, 71, 72
Hunt, Leigh, 53
Hutcheson, Francis, 42
Hutchinson, Anne, 17
Hutchinson, Thomas, ix, 17–18, 79

Indians, American, 61

James I, king of England, 13
Jay, John, 8
Jefferson, Thomas, v, 3–4, 6, 41, 66, 68, 82, 93, 94; Rush's correspondence with, 72; *Summary View,* 85
Jeffries (Jeffreys), George, 85
Jesus College, Oxford, 1
Johnson, Samuel (1696–1772), 65
Johnson, Samuel (1709–1784), 35
Jones, Reverend Hugh, 1–11; his *Present State of Virginia,* 1, 3, 7; his "Essay on the British Computation of Time, Coins, Weights, and Measures," 2; his "Panchronometer," 2; "Accidence to Christianity," 3; "Accidence to the English Tongue," 3, 6; "Accidence to Mathematics," 3
Junius, 89
Juvenal, 28, 47, 53

Kelpius, Hermit of Georgetown, 53
Kirk (Kirke), Percy, 85
Kuntze, John C., 58

Lactantius Firmianus, Lucius Caelius, 20

Laurens, Harry, 8

Laurens, Henry, 5, 7–8, 10–11; "Voyage, Capture, and Imprisonment," 8

Laurens, John, 8, 9, 10

Lawson, Deodat, 16

Lee, Arthur, 11

L'Estrange, Sir Roger, his *Seneca's Morals by Way of Abstract,* 6

Livy, 61, 62, 76

Lloyd, David, ix

Locke, John, 75, 92

Logan, James, viii, 53, 61, 93

Longinus, 72; his *On the Sublime,* 77

Lucian, 72, 89

Lucretius, 75

Luther, Martin, 57

Lutheranism, 50

Madison, James, 7, 41

Martyr, Justin, 23

Mason, George, 41

Mason, Charles, 3

Mather, Cotton, v, viii, 27, 33, 93; and witchcraft, 13–15, 16, 18–19, 22; his *Magnalia Christi Americana,* 16; *Wonders of the Invisible World,* 18; *Memorable Providences,* 18, 19

Mather, Increase, 13, 16, 18, 20, 93; President of Harvard, 17; *Essay for the Recording of Illustrious Providences,* 18; *Cases of Conscience Concerning Evil Spirits,* 18; pupil of Wigglesworth, 26, 29, 40; his account of King Philip's War, 48

Mayhew, Jonathan, 34

"Men of the Mountain" (Jacobins), 89

Middleton, Arthur, 72

Middleton, Conyers, 94

Miller, Peter, 53

Miller, Samuel, 76

Mitchell, Jonathan, 27, 32, 34

Monroe, James, 6; and Thomas Paine, 88

Montaigne, Michel Eyquem de, vii

Montesquieu, Charles de Secondat, Baron de, 92

Moore, Sir Thomas, 78

Morgan, Dr. John, 70

Morris, Gouverneur, 88, 89, 93

Motte, Andrew, viii

Muhlenberg, Ernest, 58, 62

Muhlenberg, Frederick, 62

Muhlenberg, Henry Melchior, 39, 50–63, 79; youth, 50–52; patriotism, 53; *On True Happiness,* 53; as classicist, 54–59; and interchurch relations, 60–61; during Revolution, 62

Muhlenberg, Peter, 57, 62

Nepos, 62

Newton, Sir Isaac, viii

North, Sir Thomas, his *Plutarch,* 6

Odell, Jonathan, ix

Old South Church, Boston, 14, 40

Otis, James, 82, 85, 93

Ovid, 19, 20, 23, 32, 62; *Pupula Duplex* 19; his *Amores,* 69; his *Metamorphoses,* 91

Paine, Thomas, 35, 68, 72–73, 81–96; his *Common Sense,* 62, 64, 81, 85, 87; his *Rights of Man,* 67, 88; his *Age of Reason,* 67, 88, 95; *Crisis,* 81, 85–87; background, 83–84; *New Anecdotes of Alexander the Great, Cupid and Hymen,* 85; "The Liberty-Tree," 87; "Hail Great Republic," 87; "Prospects on the Rubicon," 88; educational philosophy, 91–93; *Theophilanthropos,* 94

Pastorius, Francis Daniel, 52

Peacham, Henry, his *Garden of Rhetoric,* 28
Peale, Charles Willson, 64
Pemberton, Ebenezer, 56
Penn, William, vii, 52, 53, 61, 90, 91
Pennsylvania Hospital, 64
Pennsylvania Magazine, 84
Pericles, 85, 95
Persius, 28, 73
Peters, Dr. Samuel Andrew, 52
Petronius, 75
Phips, Sir William, 17, 22
Pindar, 37, 46
Pitt, William, 81, 88
Plantation Covenant, 27
Plato, vii, viii, 45, 46, 47, 80; Paine's admiration for, 92, 94, 95
Plautus, 28
Pliny, 19, 28, 47
Plutarch, 3, 47, 48, 78, 80
Polybius, 95
Pope, Alexander, 72
Portland, William Henry Cavendish, duke of, 88
Poulson, Zachariah, 69
Presbyterianism, 42, 43, 49
Priestley, Joseph, 75
Princeton University, 7, 41, 43, 68, 70; Presbyterian Seminary at, 79
Propertius, 33
Protesilaus, 53
Pythagoras, 46, 79

Quintilian, 29, 52; *Institutio Oratoria,* 73

Rabelais, François, 72
Ramsay, David, 9, 78
Ramsay, Martha Laurens, 9
Raynal, Guillaume Thomas François, 86
Redman, Doctor, 69
Reid, Thomas, 75

Reuss, Count Heinrich, 52, 57
Rittenhouse, David, viii, 66, 78
Robertson, William, 72
Robespierre, Maximilien François de, 88
Rodgers, Dr. John, 76
Rollin, Charles, his *Ancient History,* 10
Roman Empire, 44
Roosevelt, Theodore, 35
Royal Society, 13, 16
Rush, Benjamin, ix, 62–63, 64–80, 92; his *Autobiography,* 65; political philosophy of, 66–67; religious background of, 67–68; education of, 68–70; educational philosophy, 70–73, 80; his *Influence of Physical Causes upon the Moral Faculty,* 74; *On Natural and Medical Sciences,* 76

St. Augustine, 38, 46
Saint Paul, 46
Saratoga Convention, 8
Sarton, George, his *History of Science and the New Humanism,* viii
Schultze, Christian Emmanuel, 62
Scipio 85
Sejanus, 53
Seminole Indians, 62
Seneca, 6, 10, 42, 95; *Naturales quaestiones,* 47
Sewall, Judge Samuel, 14, 23, 27, 40, 48
Shaftesbury, Anthony Ashley Cooper, 3rd earl, 42, 75, 77
Shakespeare, William, 72
Shelburne, William Petty, 2nd earl, 8, 10
Shepard, Thomas, 27, 32, 33
Shippen, Edward, 65
Smith, Doctor James, 69
Smith, Captain John, v, 84
Socrates, viii, 45, 92, 94
Solon, 94

Sophocles, 28
Spotswood, Alexander, 1
Stamp Act, 53
Stone, Samuel, 30
Suetonius, 44, 47, 80; *Vespasian*, 44
Swift, Jonathan, 71, 72

Tacitus, 21–22, 47, 72, 75–76, 89, 92; his *Histories*, 44
Taylor, Edward, 35, 57
Tennent, William, 34
Theocritus, 28, 57
Terence, 46, 62, 75
Themistocles, 79
Theognis, 94
Thomas, Isaiah, 15
Thompson (Thomson), James, 72
Thomson, Charles, 91
Thucydides, 62, 72, 86, 89
Tompson, Benjamin, 18, 27
Trumbull, John, ix
Turgot, Anne Robert Jacques, 92
Twelve Tables, Roman legal code, 19
Tyler, Moses Coit, 8

Uhsen (Uhse), Erdman, 56
Unitarianism, 88
United States Constitution, 28
Universalism, 67
University of Pennsylvania, 64, 87
Vergil, 20, 21, 23, 47, 62, 69, 70, 72, 75; impact upon Rush, 76
Voltaire, 73
Vulgate, 33

Ward, Nathaniel, his *Simple Cobler of Aggawam*, vi
Washington, George, 5–6, 9, 10, 44, 65, 84; his Farewell Address, 62
Watts, Isaac, 42
Wayne, Anthony, 66
Webster, Peletiah, 55

Weiser, Conrad, 61
Wesley, John, 51
Whitefield, George, 52
Whitman, Walt, 81
Whittier, John Greenleaf, 12; "Calef in Boston," 12–13
Wigglesworth, Edward, father of Michael, 26
Wigglesworth, Edward, grandson of Michael, 39
Wigglesworth, Edward, son of Michael, 39
Wigglesworth, Michael, 14, 25–40, 51; *The Day of Doom*, 25, 33–34, 37, 38; early life, 26–28; *The Prayse of Eloquence*, 29; *De Microcosmo*, 29; early orations, 29; *Omnis natura inconstans est porosa*, 29; later years, 33–40; *Meat out of the Eater*, 34, 38; *God's Controversy with New England*, 38–39
Wigglesworth, Samuel, 39
William and Mary College, 1, 3, 6
Williams, Abigail, 15
Williams, Roger, 43–44
Winthrop, John, vii, viii
Winthrop, John, son of above, viii
Wise, John, 13–14, 48
Witchcraft, 12–24 *passim*, 40
Witherspoon, John, 42, 45, 70
Wolfe, General James, 84, 85
Wrangel, Charles Magnus, 52
Wythe, George, 41

Xenophon, 72, 77, 78, 94
XYZ affair, 67

Yale College, 28, 29

Zinzendorf, Count Nikolaus Ludwig von, 54
Ziegenhagen, Reverend Frederick Michael, 52